The World's Highest-Scoring Students

GLOBAL
STUDIES IN
EDUCATION

A.C. (Tina) Besley, Michael A. Peters,
Cameron McCarthy, Fazal Rizvi
General Editors

Vol. 35

The Global Studies in Education series is part of the Peter Lang Education list.
Every volume is peer reviewed and meets
the highest quality standards for content and production.

PETER LANG
New York • Bern • Berlin
Brussels • Vienna • Oxford • Warsaw

Hani Morgan

The World's Highest-Scoring Students

How Their Nations Led Them to Excellence

PETER LANG
New York • Bern • Berlin
Brussels • Vienna • Oxford • Warsaw

Library of Congress Cataloging-in-Publication Data
Names: Morgan, Hani, author.
Title: The world's highest-scoring students:
how their nations led them to excellence / Hani Morgan.
Description: New York: Peter Lang, 2018.
Series: Global studies in education; vol. 35 | ISSN 2153-330X
Includes bibliographical references.
Identifiers: LCCN 2017045803 | ISBN 978-1-4331-5142-2 (hardback: alk. paper)
ISBN 978-1-4331-5143-9 (paperback: alk. paper) | ISBN 978-1-4331-5144-6 (ebook pdf)
ISBN 978-1-4331-5145-3 (epub) | ISBN 978-1-4331-5146-0 (mobi)
Subjects: LCSH: Academic achievement—Cross-cultural studies.
Education—Cross-cultural studies. | Education and state—Cross-cultural studies.
Educational change—Cross-cultural studies.
Educational evaluation—Cross-cultural studies.
Education—United States. | Educational change—United States.
Classification: LCC LB1062.6.M67 2017 | DDC 371.26/4—dc23
LC record available at https://lccn.loc.gov/2017045803
DOI 10.3726/b12911

Bibliographic information published by **Die Deutsche Nationalbibliothek**.
Die Deutsche Nationalbibliothek lists this publication in the "Deutsche
Nationalbibliografie"; detailed bibliographic data are available
on the Internet at http://dnb.d-nb.de/.

© 2018 Peter Lang Publishing, Inc., New York
29 Broadway, 18th floor, New York, NY 10006
www.peterlang.com

TABLE OF CONTENTS

INTRODUCTION

In 1995, David Berliner and Bruce Biddle, two educational researchers with specialties in educational psychology, published *The Manufactured Crisis: Myths, Fraud, and the Attack on America's Public Schools*. Although they were psychologists who studied the dynamics of learning in the school setting, their book had very little to do with activities inside the classroom. Instead, the two researchers took a critical look at the public education enterprise in relation to the politics in which it was embedded. Their goals were to defend the system that had come under vicious attack and to change the narrative to reveal the real problems: insufficient resources for the most vulnerable students, ability grouping and tracking, and a very narrow approach to student assessment.

To set up their defense, they made three main points about student achievement: that the alleged test score declines in the 1980s and 1990s were a fiction, that students of the 1990s had outachieved their parents substantially, and that U.S. students stacked up quite well in international assessments. Their final claim was that right-wing operatives had fabricated the education crisis in order to divert attention from the nation's deepening social problems and to push schools toward market fundamentalism.

Touting the virtues of less government and blaming public school educators for supposed failures in the school system, the right's intention was to manipulate school boards, policymakers, and common citizens to accept organizational designs that promoted school choice: voucher programs, charter schools, and tuition-tax credits for those who chose private schools.

In this fine book, Hani Morgan has considered each of the concerns by Berliner and Biddle, but in doing so, he has connected the political discussion to assessing what happens at the school site and in the classroom. Like the Berliner/Biddle thesis, Morgan is interested in the dynamics that lead to student achievement. But unlike them, he does not accept the premise that the public schools in America are, overall, just doing fine. His lens is to study and compare student achievement in seven high-achieving nations with the performance of the United States. His primary method of measurement is the Program for International Student Assessment (PISA), an international test that measures 15-year-old students' reading, mathematics, and science literacy every three years. With chapters on Finland, Singapore, Japan, South Korea, China, Canada, Estonia, and the United States, Morgan asks a simple, but important question: What can the United States learn from these nations that might enhance its own education enterprise?

In answering this question, he points to links between a nation's performance on the PISA and its economic, social, and cultural health. He starts with a discussion emphasizing that world-class nations in education offer their citizens better social policies and welfare systems than the United States provides for its people. Such an approach increases the opportunities for low-income families to succeed in and contribute to society. He also looks at day-to-day practices in the schools. Take the case of Finland, considered to be among the highest-performing systems on earth. Rather than devoting too many hours for drilling children on test-taking strategies, Finland provides them with time for creative play and recess; in elementary schools, this amounts to an average of 75 minutes a day, or roughly three times as much as U.S. children get. Each school's design follows this logic, as most Finnish schoolhouses are small, functional, and airy. Also, for the Finns, norm-referenced testing is secondary, even tertiary, to helping each child develop individually.

One cannot help but compare how far the United States is behind not only in average test scores but also on sensible policies with political will that build capacity for a nation's entire population—across race, class, and region. Like the African proverb, *it takes a village to raise a child,* Morgan finds that in the highest performing countries, *it takes a caring nation—that develops an infrastructure beyond and within the school site—to educate all its children.* At the risk of oversimplification, Morgan shows beyond a reasonable doubt that high performing nations in education do not comprehend the word *tax* to be a dirty word.

He makes a convincing case that nations that invest in their youth and communities—rather than "teaching to the test" and sorting their young—improve not only their standardized test scores but also their society's overall health. This book should be required reading for any principal, teacher, parent, and citizen who cares about helping U.S. public schools improve the lives of Americans, both as well-educated individuals and as productive democratic members of society.

Thomas V. O'Brien
Professor of Educational Studies
University of Southern Mississippi

· 1 ·

WHY IT'S CRUCIAL TO LEARN FROM WORLD-CLASS NATIONS IN EDUCATION

American students have never achieved impressive results on one of the world's most important international tests, the Program for International Student Assessment (PISA). This less-than-optimal performance occurs for a variety of reasons, which involve the overall quality of America's school system and the inequalities in wealth in its society. By investigating what world-class nations in education do to achieve outstanding school systems, countries with mediocre results on international tests, such as the United States, can gain valuable insights on how they can enhance their public education system. Such insights are crucial because a nation's school system has a strong impact on the extent to which its society will thrive. For example, several studies suggest that if countries that fail to perform well on international tests raise their scores, their economies would improve (Lynch & Oakford, 2014; Paine & Schleicher, 2011).

Economic gains are just one of the advantages nations reap when they enhance the quality of their schools. In many countries, only privileged students attend outstanding schools, while those from low-socioeconomic backgrounds go to inferior institutions. Thus, when nations improve on international tests, such as the PISA, it is often after they create policies that promote equity in their school systems.

This book explores the world's leading nations in education and the methods they use to achieve outstanding test scores. It includes chapters on Finland, Singapore, Japan, South Korea, China, Canada, Estonia, and the United States. All these countries except the United States ranked among the top ten on the 2015 PISA test in at least one subject. Why include the United States if it did not achieve impressive results? For a simple reason: to compare it with the best performers.

In this introductory chapter, I discuss international tests, their critics, and the limitations of relying on these assessments to determine the quality of a nation's educational system. But first, I offer more details about how nations with mediocre educational systems can benefit by creating more opportunities for their students to improve academically. Many of these opportunities, which include creating better school systems for underprivileged students and implementing superior social policies for poor citizens, exist in world-class nations in education.

Good Schools for All Students

World-class nations in education provide superior educational opportunities for socioeconomically disadvantaged students, thus narrowing academic achievement gaps and enhancing the chances for their citizens to flourish (Lynch & Oakford, 2014; Paine & Schleicher, 2011). Unlike the United States, these nations experience smaller differences in academic achievement levels between students from low-income backgrounds and those from wealthier families. Recent PISA scores show large achievement gaps between white and low-income minority students in the United States. One study indicated that if this achievement gap were narrowed, the U.S. economy would be much stronger by 2050, expanding by $2.3 trillion (Lynch & Oakford, 2014). Another study concluded that if the United States could increase its average PISA scores by 25 points per year over 20 years, its economy would gain $41 trillion for the generation born in 2010 (Paine & Schleicher, 2011).

In addition, closing the academic achievement gap would likely mitigate the increasing racial turmoil in the United States, because it would create more equality in American society and more opportunities for low-income minority students to secure higher-paying jobs. Unfortunately, the gap in achievement that black and Hispanic students experience is huge. In 2016, for instance, three researchers from Stanford University found that for students attending the districts with the highest levels of poverty, average scores were about four grade levels lower than those of children in the wealthiest districts (Rich, Cox, & Bloch, 2016). Providing good schools and skilled teachers for low-income students, however, does not fully explain why world-class nations in education surpass the United States in international testing. More important than the school and its teachers are social policies that reduce the negative consequences involving inequalities in wealth.

Good Social Policies

When underprivileged students attend outstanding schools, the achievement gap does not necessarily narrow because schools and teachers have a limited impact on students' education. In fact, recent research analyzing over 40 million student test scores indicates that some of the wealthiest communities in the United States endure the largest achievement gaps between white and minority students (Sparks, 2016). Low-income minority students attend schools in wealthier communities because they usually live in the poorest areas of their districts. The reason these students perform less well academically involves out-of-school factors. Wealthier families are more likely to pressure their children to succeed academically, to enroll them in robotics classes, and to hire tutors (Rich et al., 2016). Other out-of-school factors that contribute to low achievement include high levels of absenteeism, exposure to family violence, lack of health care and food, and frequent moves from school to school (Berliner, 2013). Low-income students are also much more likely to be born to a teenage mother and less likely to live with both parents than their more privileged counterparts. These students suffer more social, emotional, and health problems. As a result of the financial hardships their parents face, they do not have the same opportunities to attend private preschools or to participate in enrichment activities, such as music and art (Porter, 2015). These conditions are usually more powerful toward academic achievement than the quality of the school. Some prominent researchers, such as David Berliner (2013), say that creating better social policies to reduce poverty in America is a more feasible method for reducing the academic achievement gap than merely reforming the school system:

> On average, by age 18, children and youth have spent about 10 percent of their lives in what we call schools, while spending around 90 percent of their lives in family and neighborhood. Thus, if families and neighborhoods are dysfunctional or toxic,

their chance to influence youth is nine times greater than the schools'! So it seems foolish to continue trying to affect student achievement with the most popular contemporary educational policies, mostly oriented toward teachers and schools, while assiduously ignoring the power of the outside-of-school factors. (pp. 5–6)

In the following chapters, I offer evidence showing that many world-class nations in education provide their poor citizens with superior social policies and welfare systems to reduce socioeconomic achievement gaps.

Unfortunately, there are fewer U.S. students from middle class families today than in previous years because the difference in wealth between the rich and the poor has increased considerably in the past few decades in the United States. U.S. childhood poverty rates are now the highest among OECD countries, rising by over 60% since the 1970s (Darling-Hammond, 2014). Between 1970 and 2012, the percentage of wealthy families increased from 6.6% to 15.7%, while the percentage of middle-income families decreased from 65% to 41% (Kelley, 2016). This increase in income segregation leads to fewer options for the poor to make progress. Because more wealthy families live in isolated neighborhoods, less fortunate citizens have fewer opportunities to use the resources that privileged families regularly have access to, reducing the chances to improve their condition.

Although alleviating the enormous problem of income inequality appears to be the ideal method for closing the gap in achievement, creating more equity in the American school system will also help to improve outcomes. Certain districts with large numbers of low-income students perform better academically than others, and learning from the methods such districts implement will likely narrow the achievement gap (Rabinovitz, 2016). Regrettably, there are too few of these districts. According to Stanford Professor Sean F. Reardon, schools serving large populations of low-income students rarely contain a significant number of pupils who perform at least at the national average (Boschma & Brownstein, 2016). This outcome occurs to a great extent as a consequence of the inequalities students in low-income districts encounter.

Inequalities in Schools

Schools in low-income districts suffer from a plethora of challenges, contributing to an inferior learning environment (Rich et al., 2016). As soon as children from poor families start in the U.S. public education system, they are more likely to receive a low-quality education. Even as early as the prekindergarten level, research shows this pattern to be the norm (Porter, 2015). For example, Rachel Valentino's (2015) study concluded that although high quality prekindergarten programs can narrow the achievement gap considerably, large gaps exist in the quality of prekindergarten experiences between children from low-income backgrounds and their more privileged peers.

Severe inequalities persist as students advance to higher levels. These inequalities involve a dearth of skilled teachers, textbooks, computers, and the course offerings needed to prepare students for college. Such conditions exist because the wealthiest districts typically spend three times more per student than those in the poorest areas (Darling-Hammond, 2014). Districts in poor areas function with less money as a result of the way the public school system is funded in the United States. Although in most states public schools receive money from state grants, the primary source of funds comes from local property taxes. Because most districts in poor areas are in regions where property values are low, they normally receive much less funding than those in wealthier areas (Paine & Schleicher, 2011; Porter, 2015). The world's top-performing educational systems typically do not fund their schools this way. Instead, their schools receive equitable funding, and some systems even supply more resources for the students needing them most (Darling-Hammond, 2014). In Singapore, for instance, the most skilled teachers are assigned to work with the neediest students (Paine & Schleicher, 2011).

The shortage of funds low-income districts endure does not allow them to pay teachers well, preventing them from hiring as many skilled teachers as wealthier districts have. Qualified and experienced teachers usually avoid these schools, hoping to work in districts that pay more. Novice teachers may accept a position in a low-income district but usually leave after gaining the experience that makes them more appealing to a wealthier district. As a result, schools in poor areas experience rapid turnover of faculty. Because fewer teachers want to work there, such schools often encounter more teacher shortage problems than other schools, causing them to lower their standards and to hire poorly qualified teachers. Indeed, Linda Darling-Hammond (2014) reported that teachers in high-need schools are less likely to be certified in the field they teach and more likely to have lower levels of education and lower scores on teacher licensing tests. Such conditions are usually absent in world-class nations in education. Policymakers in the United States should be concerned about these problems because teachers' experience, academic background, certification status, and teacher preparation have a considerable impact on student learning (Darling-Hammond, 2014).

High-Stakes Testing

Policymakers attempted to improve the U.S. school system in the 21st century by creating policies to hold schools and teachers accountable through high-stakes standardized tests. Unfortunately, these policies failed to reduce academic achievement gaps and created various problems that harmed socioeconomically disadvantaged students. World-class nations in education generally do not use high-stakes testing as the primary method to evaluate teachers, although some combine them with other methods of assessment (Williams & Engel, 2012). In Singapore, for example, several professionals within each school evaluate teachers on a broad range of components in addition to using test scores, and in Finland, high-stakes tests are not used *at all* to evaluate teachers (Williams & Engel, 2012).

Under the No Child Left Behind Act of 2001 (NCLB) and the 2009 Race to the Top initiative (RttP), teachers and schools faced severe consequences if their students did not score at a proficient level on tests. Schools were sometimes closed and faculty fired. Because low-income students experience many conditions that impede their chances of scoring well on tests, principals working in poor districts faced more pressure to raise these students' scores (Rose, 2015). Therefore, these pupils usually received more rote learning methods based on recall and memorization. Even if their test scores rose, they experienced a less engaging style of teaching that limited the development of higher-order thinking skills (Rose, 2015). Low-income students frequently endured not only an inferior type of teaching style but also a less stimulating classroom environment, increasing their chances of dropping out.

Fortunately, President Obama signed the Every Student Succeeds Act in December 2015, a law requiring states to use various factors for holding schools accountable rather than just test scores. While this law will likely improve the U.S. public school system, without other reforms, it will probably have little influence on many other circumstances that prevent underprivileged students from doing well on international tests.

Why Are International Tests Important?

The PISA is one of the most important international tests that students throughout the world take because unlike other international tests, it measures skills connected to workforce knowledge (Rutkowski, Rutkowski, &

Plucker, 2014). It is also offered to students in countries that make up close to 90% of the world economy, so as to compare student achievement levels internationally (Schleicher, 2011). In addition to the PISA are other valuable international tests, such as the Trends in International Mathematics and Science Study (TIMSS) and the Progress in International Reading Literacy Study (PIRLS). These tests measure the academic skills of younger students.

The Organization for Economic Co-operation and Development (OECD) offers the PISA every three years to 15-year-olds to evaluate students' skills in mathematics, science, and reading. The OECD administers this test to approximately 70 countries and economies, but the number of countries participating in a given year can vary and has increased considerably since this test was first implemented in 2000. When it was created, the PISA was designed for economically developed countries, but to make accurate comparisons, economically developing countries participate with the wealthy OECD countries. Of the 67 educational systems participating in the PISA in 2012, 34 were members of the OECD, and the rest were partner countries (Rutkowski et al., 2014).

The International Association for the Evaluation of Educational Achievement (IEA) offers the TIMSS test every four years to evaluate fourth- and eighth-grade students on their mathematics and science skills. It also offers the PIRLS test every five years to measure fourth-grade students on their reading skills. Fifty-three education systems participated in the PIRLS in 2011 (National Center for Education Statistics, 2012a), and 57 countries participated in the TIMMS at grade 4 in 2011, with 56 participating at grade 8 (National Center for Education Statistics, 2012b).

Students taking the PISA in the United States are chosen randomly from a list of all schools enrolling 15-year-old students in order to represent the entire population of students at this age. A similar process is used to select younger students for the TIMSS and the PIRLS tests. In the United States, 161 public and private schools participated on the 2012 PISA, and 6,111 students took the test (Organization for Economic Co-operation and Development [OECD], 2014). Like the PISA, both private and public schools participate in the PIRLS and the TIMMS, but generally more U.S. students take these tests. In 2011, for instance, 370 schools participated in the PIRLS, and 12,726 students took the test (National Center for Education Statistics, 2012a).

American students tend to do better on the TIMMS and the PIRLS than on the PISA. In 2011, for example, the United States ranked among the top ten countries at grade 4 on the TIMMS in science, achieving higher average scores than 47 education systems (National Center for Education Statistics, 2012b). On the PIRLS, an IEA (2012) report indicated that although U.S. students were not at the very top in 2011, they achieved a high average. However, in 2012, American students did not score among the top ten nations in any of the three subjects the PISA covers, ranking 25th in mathematics, 14th in reading, and 17th in science among the 34 member nations of the OECD (Duke, 2013). They also did not achieve impressive PISA scores in 2015 as Table 1.1 shows.

Table 1.1: Average scores of 15-year-old students on the 2015 PISA

SCIENCE	Score	READING	Score	MATHEMATICS	Score
OECD average	**493**	**OECD average**	**493**	**OECD average**	**490**
Singapore	556	Singapore	535	Singapore	564
Japan	538	Hong Kong (China)	527	Hong Kong (China)	548
Estonia	534	Canada	527	Macau (China)	544
Chinese Taipei	532	Finland	526	Chinese Taipei	542
Finland	531	Ireland	521	Japan	532
Macau (China)	529	Estonia	519	B-S-J-G (China)*	531
Canada	528	Korea, Republic of	517	Korea, Republic of	524
Vietnam	525	Japan	516	Switzerland	521
Hong Kong (China)	523	Norway	513	Estonia	520
B-S-J-G (China)*	518	New Zealand	509	Canada	516
Korea, Republic of	516	Germany	509	Netherlands	512
New Zealand	513	Macau (China)	509	Denmark	511
Slovenia	513	Poland	506	Finland	511
Australia	510	Slovenia	505	Slovenia	510
United Kingdom	509	Netherlands	503	Belgium	507
Germany	509	Australia	503	Germany	506
Netherlands	509	Sweden	500	Poland	504
Switzerland	506	Denmark	500	Ireland	504
Ireland	503	France	499	Norway	502

Belgium	502	Belgium	499	Austria	497
Denmark	502	Portugal	498	New Zealand	495
Poland	501	United Kingdom	498	Vietnam	495
Portugal	501	Chinese Taipei	497	Russian Federation	494
Norway	498	**United States**	**497**	Sweden	494
United States	**496**	Spain	496	Australia	494
Austria	495	Russian Federation	495	France	493
France	495	B-S-J-G (China)*	494	United Kingdom	492
Sweden	493	Switzerland	492	Czech Republic	492
Czech Republic	493	Latvia	488	Portugal	492
Spain	493	Czech Republic	487	Italy	490
Latvia	490	Croatia	487	Iceland	488
Russian Federation	487	Vietnam	487	Spain	486
Luxembourg	483	Austria	485	Luxembourg	486
Italy	481	Italy	485	Latvia	482
Hungary	477	Iceland	482	Malta	479
Lithuania	475	Luxembourg	481	Lithuania	478
Croatia	475	Israel	479	Hungary	477
Buenos Aires (Argentina)	475	Buenos Aires (Argentina)	475	Slovak Republic	475
Iceland	473	Lithuania	472	Israel	470
Israel	467	Hungary	470	**United States**	**470**

* China includes the 4 provinces of Beijing, Shanghai, Jiangsu, and Guangdong
Source: National Center for Education Statistics (2016).

Many researchers respect international tests because they provide data on how well American students have mastered important skills and knowledge in comparison with students in other countries. Even world leaders pay attention to these test results. For example, when President Obama learned about U.S. students' lackluster performance on the PISA in 2010, he compared it to the Sputnik crisis of the late 1950s (Ravitch, 2013).

International tests differ in an important way from the high-stakes tests that NCLB required U.S. students to take because tests like the PISA emphasize higher-order thinking skills. Such tests measure how students apply knowledge to solve new problems and how they defend their answers; however, NCLB promoted the use of tests that measured lower-level skills (Darling-Hammond, 2010). Figure 1.1 shows sample questions from the PISA.

Figure 1.1: Sample questions from the PISA

READING UNIT 1: LAKE CHAD

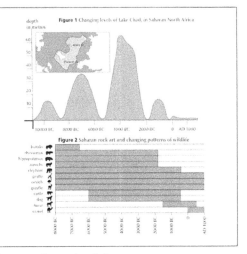

Figure 1 shows changing levels of Lake Chad, in Saharan North Africa. Lake Chad disappeared completely in about 20,000 BC, during the last Ice Age. In about 11,000 BC it reappeared. Today, its level is about the same as it was in AD 1000.

Figure 2 shows Saharan rock art (ancient drawings or paintings found on the walls of caves) and changing patterns of wildlife

Source: Past Worlds: The Times Atlas of Archaeology, Times Books Limited 1988

Use the above information about Lake Chad to answer the questions below.

QUESTION 1.1

What is the depth of Lake Chad today?

A. About two metres.

B. About fifteen metres.

C. About fifty metres.

D. It has disappeared completely.

E. The information is not provided.

QUESTION 1.2

In about which year does the graph in Figure 1 start?

....

QUESTION 1.3

Why has the author chosen to start the graph at this point?

....

....

Source: OECD (2009).

Students with high scores on international tests therefore have valuable skills, enhancing their opportunities for future success, but students with high scores on standardized tests like those NCLB required do not necessarily have these skills. To illustrate this point, a *New York Times* article described a student who passed her high school state exam on her first try and earned the designation of "Texas scholar." However, when she enrolled at the University of Houston, she failed the college entrance math exam twice. Frustrated because what she learned in public school did not prepare her for college, she transferred to a trade school (Schemo & Fessenden, 2003). Another similar case occurred when high school teachers raised students' scores for the reading section of the Texas Assessment of Academic Skills (TAAS) test through practice drills. The teachers discovered that their teaching style failed to help their students apply skills to other required reading assignments (Dodge, 2009). While these examples suggest that international tests are superior to many U.S. state tests, critics often find flaws with international tests and with the idea of using them to rank different countries.

Critics of International Tests

Recently, many prominent scholars and activists collaborated to write a letter to the director of the PISA, hoping to persuade him to stop the test. In May 2014, the *Washington Post* published a copy of the letter. The letter indicated that international assessments like the PISA promote an increase in standardized testing by pressuring policymakers to justify the use of policies similar to the Race to the Top initiative (Strauss, 2014). The letter also indicated that since the PISA is offered every three years, it encourages poor performing nations to quickly fix the problems related to inadequate test scores by implementing short-term solutions. Such an approach guarantees failure since successful school reform takes decades.

This letter also mentioned the narrow range of intelligences that standardized tests measure because these tests usually fail to evaluate the physical, civic, artistic, and moral development of students. Because OECD is an organization focusing on economic development, critics fear that it is biased toward measuring the economic potential of schools. They feel that standardized tests ignore aspects educators need to emphasize, such as preparing students to function in a democratic society and to pursue activities for personal development.

Further, those who want the PISA to end believe that OECD lacks a genuine motive for implementing the test because it has no mandate to improve the lives of children through education like UNESCO or UNICEF. They also feel this way because OECD partnered with for-profit companies that will gain financially from this partnership. The most important reason, however, that this letter mentioned for ending the PISA concerns the alleged harm it does to children. Critics believe it adds more stress on students and reduces the autonomy teachers have since it encourages the use of scripted lessons designed to prepare students for more multiple-choice tests (Strauss, 2014).

These criticisms deserve attention not only because respected scholars such as Henry Giroux, Nel Noddings, and Yong Zhao approved the letter but also because some of the concerns raised do in fact harm children. The overuse of standardized testing in the United States, for example, has caused the concerns I previously discussed when documenting how high-stakes tests impede the teaching and learning process.

However, the PISA does not cause stress to children nearly as much as the testing implemented during the NCLB act and the RttP initiative. Whereas NCLB and RttP required all public schools to test students on a yearly basis, the PISA is offered only once every three years to considerably fewer students. As I pointed out earlier, only 6,111 U.S. students took the PISA in 2012, a very small sample considering that the total number of American students in a given grade is in the millions. Statistics published in 2012, for example, indicate that the total number of U.S. students enrolled in the 10th grade, the grade in which most students take the PISA, was 3,809,972 (Snyder & Dillow, 2012). It is unlikely that a school will devote much time to prepare students to take the PISA because there is a low chance that its students will be chosen to take it.

The PISA provides crucial data about the world's educational systems, data that can be used to transform the systems of poorer performing countries into world-class nations in education. For example, an analysis of a recent PISA test revealed that American schools with very low levels (fewer than 10%) of socioeconomically disadvantaged students achieved higher scores than many of the top-performing nations on the PISA, including Finland, Japan, and Korea (Ravitch, 2013). Such information suggests that the United States could easily become a leading nation in education if the conditions that low-income students encounter in school and society improve.

In her book on the privatization movement in the United States, Diane Ravitch (2013) criticized the tests used during NCLB and RttP for labeling, grading, and ranking teachers, students, schools, and principals. However, she mentioned that certain tests, when used wisely, can provide important information:

> Tests may be useful when they are used appropriately. They should be used to gather information about schools and districts so that programs may be assessed. They should be used for diagnostic purposes, to determine which students need more help with specific problems. They should be used to establish trends. The best tests have no stakes attached to them. The National Assessment of Educational Progress is an exemplar. It tests samples of students. No one knows who will take it. No one can prepare for it. No single student takes the entire test. No individual or school is punished or rewarded because of the scores on NAEP. (p. 263)

The PISA has many characteristics of the NAEP, and it lacks many components of the kind of standardized testing that harms students. It is true that the PISA ranks countries, focuses on academic subjects, and does not emphasize other important aspects of education like the physical, artistic, and moral development of students. However, PISA analyses vary from year to year and have recently explored some of the areas critics say it overlooks. For instance, for the first time, the PISA recently conducted a survey on the level of student happiness in various countries (OECD, 2013).

Although the PISA and other international tests are better than many other assessments, using these tests is not an exact science. Errors can occur when the tests are scored, and inappropriate comparisons can and do happen. Additionally, it is very difficult to translate content from one language to another for students in two different countries to experience an equivalent test (Bracey, 2009). International tests, therefore, need to be used with other methods to evaluate students, teachers, and school systems accurately.

Creativity

Critics sometimes object to using international assessments because some of the top-performing countries in testing lack people with creativity and entrepreneurial skills. They argue that the approach to teaching and learning in places like China and Singapore prevents schools from producing people with these skills, thwarting the chances for these areas of the world to produce many innovations. In 2008, for example, the world's leading patent offices recognized only 473 innovations from China compared with 14,399 from the United States (Zhao, 2012a).

When China's outstanding PISA scores were announced in 2010, rather than celebrate enthusiastically, many Chinese people viewed these scores with caution. A considerable number of Chinese people believe that the intense effort at acquiring the knowledge that enables Chinese students to do well on exams is problematic because it thwarts creativity (Zhao, 2012b). Chinese students generally outperform others as a result of the approach to education used in China. Doing well on the college entrance exam, known as the *gaoko*, is paramount for students, and parents prepare children for performing well on tests before kindergarten. They spend huge sums of money on tutoring. All schools, even at the kindergarten level, spend considerable time preparing students to take the tests needed to advance to higher grade levels until they have to take the most important one: the *gaoko*.

Professor Yong Zhao says that the Chinese educational system contributes to the country's lack of creativity for various reasons. First, because students devote all their time to academic excellence, they have little or no time to pursue anything that does not help them do well on tests. The little time students spend on activities unrelated to academic work minimizes their chances to experiment and deprives them of developing entrepreneurial and creative talent. Second, those who have creative and entrepreneurial skills but do not have good test-taking skills will likely not prosper. The reason for this outcome is that the Chinese system rewards good test takers by allowing them access to better jobs while denying prestige and resources to those who perform poorly on tests (Zhao, 2012b). In addition to China and Singapore, other East Asian nations, such as South Korea and Japan, are at times criticized for their lack of creativity as a result of the regimented approach to education these nations often use.

Although some top-performing nations in international testing may lack creativity, others use methods designed to promote it. An exemplar is Finland. Like Singapore, Japan, South Korea, and China, Finland has achieved some of the highest scores on the PISA in the 21st century, but this nation differs from the East Asian top performers in many ways in its pedagogical approach. One way Finland differs relates to its commitment to enhance creativity. Rather than devote great effort to transmit a mammoth amount of knowledge in children, schools in Finland devote greater value to problem solving, the arts, and creativity (Ravitch, 2013). One theme of this book relates to how world-class nations in education can vary greatly in their approach to education. Another theme involves borrowing practices from abroad cautiously. Although some top-performing countries implement certain policies that would dramatically improve U.S. schools, some of their other methods would worsen the American system.

How Will This Book Differ from Others?

I believe this book offers a new perspective in several ways. First, it provides a balanced view of the highest-ranking nations in education that not only documents the outstanding practices they use to achieve stellar results but also points out the problems they endure. It also describes the most recent practices that various nations have used to remain the best performers and the strategies that others have implemented to climb to the top. Whereas previous authors selected world-class countries in education based on their 2012 PISA scores, I used the 2015 PISA scores for this purpose.

References

Berliner, D. (2013). Effects of inequality and poverty vs. teachers and schooling on America's youth. *Teachers College Record*. Retrieved from http://www.tcrecord.org/content.asp?contentid=16889

Boschma, J., & Brownstein, R. (2016, February 29). The concentration of poverty in American schools. *The Atlantic*. Retrieved from http://www.theatlantic.com/education/archive/2016/02/concentration-poverty-american-schools/471414/

Bracey, G. (2009). The big tests: What ends do they serve? *Educational Leadership, 66*(3), 32–37.

Darling-Hammond, L. (2010). Restoring our schools. *Nation, 290*(23), 14–20.

Darling-Hammond, L. (2014). What can PISA tell us about U.S. education policy? *New England Journal of Public Policy, 26*(1), 1–14.

Dodge, A. (2009). Heuristics and NCLB standardized tests: A convenient lie. *International Journal of Progressive Education, 5*(2), 6–22.

Duke, D. (2013). Are we pushing for greatness? *Phi Delta Kappan, 94*(5), 45–49.

International Association for the Evaluation of Educational Achievement. (2012). *PIRLS 2011 international results in reading.* Chestnut Hill, MA: TIMMS & PIRLS International Study Center.

Kelley, S. (2016, June 23). Mixed-income neighborhoods face steady decline. *Cornell Chronicle*. Retrieved from http://www.news.cornell.edu/stories/2016/06/mixed-income-neighborhoods-face-steady-decline

Lynch, R. G., & Oakford, P. (2014). *The economic benefits of closing educational achievement gaps: Promoting growth and strengthening the nation by improving the educational outcomes of children of color.* Washington, DC: Center for American Progress. Retrieved from https:// cdn.americanprogress.org/wp-content/uploads/2014/11/WinningEconomy Report2.pdf

National Center for Education Statistics. (2012a). *Highlights from PIRLS 2011.* Retrieved from http://nces.ed.gov/pubs2013/2013010.pdf

National Center for Education Statistics. (2012b). *Highlights from TIMSS 2011.* Retrieved from http://nces.ed.gov/pubs2013/2013009rev.pdf

National Center for Education Statistics. (2016). *Performance of U.S. 15-year-old students in science, reading, and mathematics literacy in an international context: First look at PISA 2015.* Retrieved from https://nces.ed.gov/pubs2017/2017048.pdf

Organization for Economic Co-operation and Development. (2009). *Take the test: Sample questions from OECD's PISA assessments.* Paris: Organization of Economic Cooperation and Development.

Organization for Economic Co-operation and Development. (2013). *PISA 2012 results: Ready to learn: Students' engagement, drive and self-beliefs (Vol. III).* Paris: Organization of Economic Co-operation and Development.

Organization for Economic Co-operation and Development. (2014). *How your school compares internationally: Natick High School.* Paris: Organization of Economic Cooperation and Development.

Paine, S. L., & Schleicher, A. (2011). *What the US can learn from the world's most successful education reform efforts.* New York, NY: McGraw-Hill Research Foundation.

Porter, E. (2015, September 22). Education gap between rich and poor is growing wider. *The New York Times.* Retrieved from http://www.nytimes.com/2015/09/23/business/economy/education-gap-between-rich-and-poor-is-growing-wider.html?smid=fb-nytimes&smtyp=cur&_r=1

Rabinovitz, J. (2016, April 29). Local education inequities across U.S. revealed in new Stanford data set. *Stanford Graduate School of Education.* Retrieved from https://ed.stanford.edu/news/local-education-inequities-across-us-revealed-new-stanford-data-set

Ravitch, D. (2013). *Reign of error: The hoax of the privatization movement and the danger to America's public schools.* New York, NY: Knopf.

Rich, M., Cox, A., & Bloch, M. (2016, April 29). Money, race and success: How your school district compares. *The New York Times.* Retrieved from http://www.nytimes.com/interactive/2016/04/29/upshot/money-race-and-success-how-your-school-district-compares.html?_r=1

Rose, M. (2015). School reform fails the test. *The American Scholar, 84*(1), 18–30.

Rutkowski, D., Rutkowski, L., & Plucker, J. A. (2014). Should individual U.S. schools participate in PISA? *Phi Delta Kappan, 96*(4), 68–73.

Schemo, J. D., & Fessenden, F. (2003, December 3). A miracle revisited: Measuring success; Gains in Houston schools: How real are they? *The New York Times.* Retrieved from http://www.ny-times.com/2003/12/03/us/a-miracle-revisited-measuring-success-gains-in-houston-schools-how-real-are-they.html

Schleicher, A. (2011). Is the sky the limit to education improvement? *Phi Delta Kappan, 93*(2), 58–63.

Snyder, T. D., & Dillow, S. A. (2012). *Digest of education statistics 2011*. Washington, DC: National Center for Education Statistics.

Sparks, S. D. (2016, May 10). Study: Most school districts have achievement gaps. *Education Week*. Retrieved from http://www.edweek.org/ew/articles/2016/05/11/study-most-school-districts-have-achievement-gaps.html

Strauss, V. (2014, May 13). Academics call for pause in PISA tests. *The Washington Post*. Retrieved from https://www.washingtonpost.com/news/answer-sheet/wp/2014/05/13/academics-call-for-pause-in-pisa-tests/

Valentino, R. A. (2015). Will public pre-k really close achievement gaps? Gaps in prekindergarten quality between students and across states. *Center for Education Policy Analysis*. Retrieved from https://cepa.stanford.edu/sites/default/files/Valentino%20RA_Quality%20Gaps%20Paper%2015_0515.pdf

Williams, J., & Engel, L. C. (2012). How do other countries evaluate teachers? *Phi Delta Kappan, 94*(4), 53–57.

Zhao, Y. (2012a). Flunking innovation and creativity. *Phi Delta Kappan, 94*(1), 56–61.

Zhao, Y. (2012b). *World class learners: Educating creative and entrepreneurial students*. Thousand Oaks, CA: Corwin.

· 2 ·

EDUCATION IN FINLAND

The Closest We Can Get to a Utopian System

If two parents asked me which school system in the world provides the best learning environment for children, I would boldly say that Finland does. Although Finland failed to score highest in any subject on the 2015 PISA and even performed less well than it had in previous years, students there continued to do better than those in most other countries. As I discussed in Chapter 1, scores on international tests do not provide feedback on many crucial components involving the education of students. Some educators believe Finland addresses more critical elements of education better than any other country.

How did Finland do on the 2015 PISA? Students there ranked 5th in science, 4th in reading, and 12th in math, scoring significantly higher than the United Sates in each subject (Heim, 2016). In previous years, Finland performed even better. In 2009, for instance, Finland ranked 2nd in science, 3rd in reading, and 5th in math (Stewart, 2012). Although Finland has declined somewhat, it is not necessarily due to lower-quality teaching. Other countries may have started teaching to the test. I will offer more reasons for Finland's decline at the end of this chapter.

Outstanding Educational Practices

Finland's high scores reflect the superior practices students experience shortly before they start school. Some of the practices that promote learning there include providing students with more time for play and more time to develop their critical thinking skills than other countries allow. The Finns also excel in providing students with special needs the guidance they deserve to succeed academically. In addition, like many other top-performing countries, they permit only their most qualified high school students to enroll in their rigorous teacher education programs.

Adequate Time for Play and Recess

Rather than emphasize reading and math, Finnish day care centers focus on creative play. The purpose of this approach of early childhood education is to encourage the health of children (Butler, 2016). Preschool children in the United States enjoyed a similar environment about 20 years ago, but in more recent years, they have endured a more didactic approach designed to boost their academic performance (Kohn, 2015). Little, if any, evidence supports such an approach. In fact, starting didactic education too early could impede academic development rather than enhance it. For example, in a study involving 343 children, Rebecca A. Marcon found that children exposed to more didactic instruction in preschool got lower grades in elementary school than those who received more chances to learn from play (Kohn, 2015).

The increased opportunities to play in Finland continue as children enter elementary school. Elementary schools there average 75 minutes a day of recess, almost 3 times as much as the 27 minutes elementary schools in the United States average (Abrams, 2011). Rebecca Marcon's study is not the only one suggesting that movement and play benefit students. The Centers for Disease Control and Prevention (2010) reported that 50 studies suggest positive relationships between academic performance and physical activity. Researchers from North Carolina, for example, concluded that students who took 10-minute breaks with physical activity focused more on learning after their break than their counterparts who took more sedentary breaks (Conyers & Wilson, 2015).

Some of the factors that led American schools to devote less time for play and recess were programs like NCLB and RttP (Abrams, 2011; Kohn, 2015). These programs led schools to spend excessive time preparing students for standardized testing. Such an approach not only prevents teachers from teaching in a way to develop strong thinking skills but also discourages educators from permitting students to experience the play and movement they need for healthy childhood development.

No Standardized Tests to Evaluate Students or Teachers

In addition to leaving students with less time for play, the overuse of standardized tests has many drawbacks. It leads teachers to teach to the test, promotes a mechanical style of learning, puts unnecessary pressure on students, and leads to cheating problems when implemented as the only method to measure student learning. Many parents and teachers in the United States experienced these consequences in the 21st century because American policies required schools and teachers to be held accountable primarily through such tests. Finland uses very few of these tests, only for curricular decisions and university admission and not for student and teacher assessment (Williams & Engel, 2012).

How are students and teachers evaluated in Finland? Rather than use statistical indicators, student progress is measured through each student's individual development. Educational leaders believe that learning should determine teachers' practice, not students' standardized test scores. Academic performance is the school's responsibility and not that of external assessors. Because the teaching force consists of the most skilled professionals in their field, they are the ones believed to be most fit to evaluate academic performance. Consequently, it is the teachers themselves who create tests to assess students (Partanen, 2011). They typically provide feedback to students in narrative format to describe progress in learning and areas needing improvement (Darling-Hammond, 2011/2012). All students receive their report card at the end of each grading period. Of course there are limitations in comparing student progress when using such an approach, but Finnish educators believe these limitations outweigh the problems standardized testing causes in the United States and in other countries as well (Darling-Hammond & Rothman, 2015).

As for the teachers, educational leaders trust that their strong preparation in and commitment to teaching are the most important components that will lead them to perform well:

> There is no formal teacher evaluation in Finland. Teachers receive feedback from the school principal and the school staff itself. Because Finland does not have a standardized assessment for evaluating students, there is no formal consideration of student

learning outcomes in the evaluation. Teacher and leader effectiveness are defined using a broader meaning of student learning than just scores in mathematics and reading literacy.

Once a teacher has permanent employment in a school, there are no checkpoints or means for terminating a contract unless there is a violation of the ethical rules of teaching. Finland relies on the strong preparation of teachers, their professional ethic, and their opportunities for ongoing engagement with colleagues in the professional work of teaching and curriculum and assessment development to support their effectiveness. A good teacher is one who is able to help all children progress and grow in a holistic way. (Darling-Hammond & Rothman, 2015, p. 37)

Strong Commitment to Students with Special Needs

Equally important to the practice of avoiding standardized tests to assess students is the practice of creating optimal learning conditions for students with special needs. Educators in Finland believe it is crucial to provide special education as early as possible. Consequently, they diagnose learning problems during the early childhood years and place more students in special needs programs than many other nations do (Sahlberg, 2012).

In addition to helping students excel academically, the strong emphasis on helping students with special needs lowers the grade repetition rate. In fact, Finland's grade repetition rate is considerably lower than those of many European nations. Fewer than 2% of students who complete compulsory school at the age of 16 repeat a grade (Välijärvi & Sahlberg, 2008). Repeating a grade is costly and inefficient. Students usually are not weak in all subjects, so repeating only the subjects they are weak in is a better solution. Repeating a grade may also be embarrassing to students and can turn them into reluctant learners (Sarjala, 2013).

The higher number of students in special education programs also means that students with special needs will less likely withstand the humiliation associated with being placed in such a program. They do not stand out as much from the rest of the students as in countries with fewer special needs students do because many of them get assigned to such a program. As many as one third of all the students in Finland's compulsory school system received some form of special education during the 2009–2010 school year (Sahlberg, 2012).

In comparison with Finland, the United States does not do as much in diagnosing weak students in the early grades and providing them with the guidance to succeed in the subjects that frustrate them. Consequently, many parents struggle to determine the reasons their children have problems in certain subjects. The failure to diagnose students with reading problems in the early years of schooling in the United States harms students in later years. Unfortunately, preschool and elementary teachers in the United States usually do not get trained to diagnose children who show signs of reading disorders. Failure to do so means that students who need remediation will likely not get it when they need it most—between ages 3 to 7. These are the years when it is paramount for students to develop the reading skills needed to succeed in later years (Kinlan, 2011).

Another advantage of Finland's approach involves flexibility. Students do not need a formal diagnosis to receive special education (Björn, Aro, Koponen, Fuchs, & Fuchs, 2016). Children get the support they need soon after teachers suspect they need it. In comparison, special education services in the United States are bureaucratic and rigid, leading many parents to have unpleasant experiences with them (Kinlan, 2011).

The Finns use two methods in comprehensive schools for placing students in special education programs. The first involves leaving students in their regular classes but providing them with a special education teacher. The students with special needs work in small groups part of the time under the supervision of the special education teacher. The second method involves placing students in a separate class in their school or sometimes in a separate institution (Sahlberg, 2012).

Outstanding Teacher Preparation

Students with special needs are not the only ones who reap the benefits of working with a teacher with expertise. Those not needing a special program are also taught by highly skilled professionals chosen from the brightest people in the country. Indeed, candidates hoping to enter a teacher education program must complete a rigorous two-stage process:

> The first stage is a review of documents. Applicants don't get beyond this stage unless they score well on the national college entrance exams and have a high grade point average and a strong record of nonacademic accomplishments in high school. In the second stage of the review, the applicant must excel on a demanding written exam on assigned books in pedagogy; pass an expert observation of their social and communication skills; and perform well in a demanding interview conducted by experienced educators who ask, among other things, why the candidate wants to become a teacher. (Tucker, 2012, p. 42)

The Finns accept only 1 out of every 10 applicants into their teacher education institutions, thereby recruiting the best students from their high schools. In the United States, the standards are much lower. In 2012, for example, Marc Tucker mentioned the following:

> The most recent data from the College Board show that college applicants planning to go to schools of education scored in the bottom one-third on their SATs. Their combined mathematics and reading scores were 57 points below the national average. (Tucker, 2012, p. 42)

The teacher preparation programs in Finland include at least four characteristics that differentiate them from many other programs in the world: a rigorous master's degree, a research component, a strong focus on pedagogical content knowledge, and a strong clinical element (OECD, 2011).

A Five-Year Master's Degree

Whereas in the United States teachers typically enter the teaching profession with a four-year degree, in Finland they need a five-year master's degree. As discussed previously, the admissions process is extremely selective. For example, over 6,600 students applied in 2010 for the 660 available slots in primary school preparation programs. Teachers at the primary level major in education but also need to minor in at least two subjects taught in the primary school curriculum. Upper grade teachers major in the subject they will teach but also do the work needed to teach their content well.

Research Skills

Teacher candidates learn to make decisions based on research. They not only gain familiarity of research in human development but also acquire research skills themselves, allowing them to complete the thesis required for the master's degree. Students studying to be primary grade teachers usually focus on a topic involving pedagogy, while those preparing to be upper grade teachers typically select a topic related to their subject area.

Pedagogical Content Knowledge

Teachers in Finland have skills not only on how to do research but also on how to apply it into their practice. They know how to deal with issues in teaching from a variety of disciplines, including educational psychology, sociology, special-needs education, assessment, and curriculum theories. Prospective primary and upper grade teachers are prepared well for subject-specific pedagogy rather than in the generic manner common in many mediocre teacher education programs.

A Strong Clinical Element

Before students complete their teacher preparation programs, they need to have a minimum of a full year of clinical experience. Students do this practical training, which consists of observing and practice teaching, in a school under the supervision of faculty with advanced credentials in education. These programs aim to model innovative practices. Students also problem solve as they participate in planning, action, and reflection.

No shortcuts to the rigorous teacher preparation programs are allowed. The only organizations in Finland that can issue teacher licenses are universities (Sahlberg, 2011). Finland does not have programs such as Teach for America like the United States or Teach First available in some European nations (Sahlberg, 2013). In some regions of the United States, a considerable number of teachers enter the teaching profession through an alternative program. During the 21st century, for example, there was a time when approximately half of all new teachers in Florida entered the teaching profession through an alternative certification program (Lips & Ladner, 2009).

This approach of entering the teaching profession is problematic because such programs vary greatly in quality, with research showing mixed results on their effectiveness. Some studies show that teachers starting their careers as alternative route candidates perform less well in their first two years on the job than their fully prepared counterparts. However, studies also show that some experienced teachers who complete selective alternative route programs help their students make more academic gains than other teachers with similar experience (Darling-Hammond, 2009).

More problematic than the great differences in quality among alternative route programs are the high attrition rates associated with them. One study, for example, showed that only 14.8% of Teach for America (TFA) teachers continued to teach in their original school after their fourth year. This statistic is alarming considering that the United States has high teacher attrition rates in the education sector, with even higher levels in low-income districts where TFA teachers get recruited to teach for their first two years (Donaldson & Johnson, 2011).

In Finland, on the other hand, teacher attrition is not a problem. Teachers usually stay in the same school for life, and very few primary teachers leave their profession after the first five years. Only about 10% to 15% of teachers leave the profession (Darling-Hammond & Rothman, 2015).

The Teaching Profession in Finland

The profession of teaching is respected greatly in Finland because it takes great skill to become a teacher and because few people are chosen. In addition, completing a degree from a teacher preparation program makes people competitive in the Finnish labor market. To illustrate this point, Pasi Sahlberg (2013) explained that the Finnish finance minister held a primary school teaching degree. Indeed, holding a degree from a teacher preparation program in Finland compares with graduating with a degree in medicine, law, architecture, and engineering. The social status Finnish teachers receive is so strong that one opinion survey involving 1,300 adults revealed that Finnish males believed that a teacher was the most desirable spouse to have out of a list of 30 professions. Although the women participating in the survey identified a medical doctor as their most desirable spouse, a teacher still ranked highly, coming in third as the most desirable profession (Darling-Hammond & Rothman, 2015).

One distinguishing feature of the teaching profession in Finland involves the power teachers enjoy in making decisions toward the education of children. Teachers are provided with high levels of autonomy as a result of the trust they earn from members of society. This trust was evident in the 1980s when a high level of authority for education was devolved from the Ministry of Education to municipalities and schools. This trend occurred in part from the skepticism toward central organizations with regard to their knowledge of what works best in schools (OECD, 2011).

Although teachers in Finland enjoy more respect and more autonomy than those in many other countries, they do not get paid especially well. However, they do make slightly more than the OECD average when their earnings are compared with those of workers with similar educational backgrounds (Startz, 2016). On the other hand, the United States falls below the OECD average in this category.

In comparison with other countries, teachers in Finland assign less homework. Students spend only about half an hour a day on homework. Finnish teachers also spend less time teaching than their counterparts in other nations. A middle school teacher averages only 600 hours annually in Finland, but a teacher at a similar level in the United States averages 1,080 hours (Darling-Hammond & Rothman, 2015).

Consequently, teachers do some of their most important work when they are not teaching. For example, they participate in selecting textbooks, developing syllabi, deciding on course offerings, developing curriculum and assessments, and planning and scheduling professional development (Wei, Andree, & Darling- Hammond, 2009).

The high level of autonomy teachers experience not only makes their profession more enjoyable but also creates more opportunities for them to teach effectively. The time they have resulting from the fewer hours they teach allows for more collaboration. In many European nations, including Finland, Hungary, Denmark, Italy, Norway, and Switzerland, schools provide considerable time for regular collaboration among teachers on various aspects of instruction including lesson planning. In the United States, teachers usually have only three to five hours per week for lesson planning, which they normally do independently (Wei et al., 2009). The schools in the United States that have experimented with increasing their levels of collaboration, including collective planning, peer coaching, jointly evaluating student work, and working in teams, have enjoyed more success, especially in high-need schools (Chenoweth, 2009; Darling-Hammond, 2006).

In Finland, teaching is inextricably linked to leadership because all principals need to be qualified to teach at their school, and most choose to teach. This approach promotes trust and professionalism between the teachers and principals (Sahlberg, 2011). To become a principal, a candidate needs to complete the appropriate academic training at a university. This training usually occurs part time as the candidate teaches at a school. Education authorities typically select the candidates they believe will be good principals with the approval of the teachers (Darling-Hammond & Rothman, 2015).

Superior Social Policies

Finland's educational system is linked to the country's strong social policies. Each school in the compulsory system provides students with a free meal every day and free health care services. Schools include nurses, dentists, psychologists, and social workers. Pupils also receive free school transportation if the school is far from home (Finnish National Board of Education, 2016). One reason the country has such a successful educational system involves the lack of inequalities in its schools and society.

Students in low-income areas in the United States usually attend inferior schools. In some cases, parents pay large sums of money to send their children to private schools, hoping to avoid enrolling them in the inferior schools located in their districts. These two situations do not occur in Finland because all children attend good schools regardless of their socioeconomic backgrounds and because no private schools exist in Finland. Even the few independent schools in Finland are free. All education in Finland is public. Whether students are in a university studying for a Ph.D. or in the noncompulsory school system makes no difference. It is all free (Partanen, 2011).

The PISA surveys show how equitable the public school system in Finland is. The first PISA survey in 2000 indicated that among all OECD nations, Finland had the smallest performance variations among its schools in science, math, and reading. This trend reoccurred in 2003 and became stronger in 2006 and 2009 (Sahlberg, 2012).

Finland borrowed many social policies from its Scandinavian neighbors, particularly Sweden. Although the idea of the comprehensive school emerged in Finland, the Finns used many aspects of the Swedish welfare state (OECD, 2011). The Finns' commitment to children's well-being manifests itself in the design of the school buildings, which are usually small, functional, and airy, making it easy for teachers to implement the personalized attention they are known for. As a result of the trust parents have in teachers and the strong commitment to helping struggling students in school, Finland has one of the world's lowest rates of children who receive private tutoring (Dizik, 2014).

Historical Background

Finland was not a leading country in education for many years. Although its new educational system was implemented in the early 1970s, it took 20 years for the reforms put into place to lead to the dramatic improvement we see today. American reformers can learn a great deal from Finland's reform movement because this nation used a philosophy and methods the United States usually overlooks. For example, the charter schools and competition that have increased in the 21st century in the United States do not exist in Finland. So how did Finland rise to the top in education? A historical look sheds light on what happened to transform its educational system into one of the best in the world.

Finland's Education System in the 1950s

Shortly after World War II, severe inequalities in educational opportunities existed in Finland. Only children residing in towns or larger municipalities could go to grammar or middle schools (OECD, 2011; Sahlberg, 2012). Two kinds of schools existed—civic schools and grammar schools. Students in civic schools pursued vocational education, which could lead to vocational training. This training, however, like the education in grammar schools, was available only in larger municipalities and towns. Students in grammar schools pursued five years of schooling, helping them to attend an academic high school that prepared them to enter a university. The relatively small number of students who enrolled in grammar schools shows how limited educational opportunities were. In 1950, for instance, only 27% of 11-year-old children in Finland enrolled in these schools (Sahlberg, 2012), and two-thirds of these schools were privately governed (OECD, 2011). Teaching at this time was teacher centered and formal.

The ideas for creating Finland's current system emerged during the postwar era. Parliament created several reform commissions during this time. One of these commissions offered the vision of a new type of school that would serve all students, but grammar school teachers and universities opposed this recommendation, resulting in its rejection in 1946.

About a decade later, the Commission on School Programs recommended this idea again, arguing for compulsory education to occur in a nine-year comprehensive school that would require public and private schools to merge. Although there was debate as to whether all students could be educated at the same level and as to whether society needed all students to be educated to such a level, the need for equality grew. Consequently, the Finnish parliament created legislation in 1968 for a new educational system founded on a comprehensive school for students in grades 1–9 (OECD, 2011).

The transformation from the old system to the new one was challenging and slow. In an interview about the challenges of creating the new system, Jukka Sarjala, who worked in the Ministry of Education and became the Director-General of the National Board of Education, said that many municipalities resisted the new system. The resistance resulted because teachers were unaccustomed to teaching children with different backgrounds in the same classrooms. After a few years, as the older teachers retired, the reforms were eventually accepted. In 1972, Finland implemented *peruskoulu*, a new nine-year compulsory education system that was designed to reduce many inequalities the old system created (OECD, 2011).

The new system was first implemented in northern Finland, later spreading to the municipalities in the southern part of the country. Children would no longer be separated into two streams like in the old system. Pasi Sahlberg (2012), one of the leading authors on education in Finland, argued that comprehensive school reform created three components that would later prove to be crucial in developing a well-performing system: equal opportunity, career counseling, and highly-qualified teachers.

Providing more students with opportunities to be educated created more equality. However, teaching students with different backgrounds at once meant that a new approach of education would be needed. Because there would be an increase in the variety of students, teachers would need to differentiate instruction to create equal opportunities for students to succeed, and students with weak skills would need special education programs.

Career counseling, like special education, became an essential part of the school curriculum. Counseling was vital to prevent students from making poor choices after they graduated from the nine-year compulsory system. Today, the three choices students can make after graduating include (1) continuing in vocational upper secondary education, (2) continuing in general upper secondary education, or (3) finding a job.

Teachers in the new system would also need more expertise to teach the wider variety of students that would be present in their classrooms. They would need to provide alternative methods of teaching. This requirement meant that teacher preparation programs would need to be more rigorous.

Upper Secondary Education

The increased opportunities for students to get an education that the new compulsory school system created led to the need for students to be able to continue their education. In 1970, less than half of adults in Finland obtained an upper secondary degree (OECD, 2011). Today, over 99% of students complete *peruskoulu*, and approximately 95% continue in upper secondary schools. Over 90% complete the certification needed to pursue higher education (Sahlberg, 2012). The increase in the number of students who finish upper secondary school resulted in part from the reforms enacted in 1985, allowing for a new and much more flexible system that created more choice (OECD, 2011).

Upper secondary education promotes choice in several ways. First, students who pursue it have the option to choose between general or vocational education. Vocational upper secondary education prepares students between the ages of 16 and 19 for numerous occupations. Students who choose this option need to spend at least six months of on-the-job learning in a real work setting. Second, students in upper secondary school do not take classes according to age groups and benefit from personalized learning plans. Schools at this level use modular curriculum units that allow students to take courses at their own pace. Thus, some students complete their studies much faster than others do.

Challenges for Future Success

Although many aspects of Finland's education system deserve attention and even emulation, like any country, Finland faces challenges that need to be addressed. One of these involves the country's recent decline in PISA scores. On the 2012 PISA, Finland's scores in math slipped out of the top 10 for the first time. This slide continued on the 2015 PISA when its scores dropped 5 points in reading, 10 points in math, and 11 points in science as all the other top-performing countries except Vietnam scored slightly higher or maintained similar scores (Heim, 2016).

In an interview for *Education Week*, Pasi Sahlberg offered his insights on what caused Finland's lower scores on the 2012 PISA. He mentioned that one reason Finland had declined involved its lack of effort in improving students' mathematics scores as other countries took more steps to improve theirs. Dr. Sahlberg also explained that huge numbers of foreigners visited the successful Finnish schools, making authorities fearful of changing anything. Another reason involved the increasing number of non-Finnish speaking immigrants who came to Finland (Tucker, 2014).

During a more recent interview with the *Washington Post*, Dr. Sahlberg provided a few more explanations for Finland's decline. The first has to do with the drop in the educational performance of boys in recent years. He explained that this drop is stronger in Finland than in any other OECD country.

In fact, Finland is the only country where boys significantly underperform when compared with girls in all three subjects the PISA assesses—reading, math, and science. In reading, the drop is believed to be due to the diminished role of reading for pleasure among boys.

Dr. Sahlberg also believes that the increasing use of the Internet in Finland is having adverse effects on learning. Students there spend over four hours a day on the Internet and experience increased distractibility and shallow levels of information processing.

Finally, the economic downturn Finland has endured in recent years has influenced the education sector more than other sectors, forcing many municipalities to increase class sizes and merge schools. The downturn has caused schools to reduce spending, professional development, and school improvement. As a result, Finland has recently experienced a lower number of classroom assistants, support staff, and special education personnel (Heim, 2016).

The different achievement levels in reading between boys and girls is one of the few areas that Finland can improve by modeling some of the methods the United States currently implements. Finland had the largest gender gap of any country in reading on the 2012 PISA, with females outscoring males by an average of 62 points, but the United States' gender gap was twice as low. This gap means that Finland's high scores in reading depended entirely on their females' performance because their males' score of 494 was only slightly above the OECD average for males (Loveless, 2015). The United States, unlike many other OECD countries, has more awareness of gender-related differences that affect achievement in reading. As the United States has implemented programs to close this gap, other countries, such as Finland, appear to be slow to respond (Brozo & Crain, 2016).

The causes for the gender gap in reading are debatable. Because this gap exists across the globe regardless of differences in child rearing practices and methods of education, educators often argue that the gap is biological. However, evidence also exists that refutes the biological explanation. For example, according to students' scores on the National Assessment of Educational Progress (NAEP), a national test given to elementary and secondary students in the United States, the gender gap has been shrinking. The NAEP results reveal that this gap is half of what it was 40 years ago for nine-year-olds (Loveless, 2015). This statistic strongly suggests that schools can ameliorate gender gaps in academic achievement.

Induction of New Teachers and Professional Development

In addition to a teaching approach that may promote large gender differences in PISA reading scores are two other areas of Finland's school system that could be improved. Although Finland's teacher preparation program is uniform, the induction of new teachers is not. Professional development programs are problematic as well.

Some schools offer advanced methods to support new staff, but other schools merely welcome new teachers and wish them luck in their new position. Additionally, in some schools, the principals are responsible for teacher induction, but in others, experienced teachers are responsible for this job (Sahlberg, 2011). With regard to professional development, there is a lack of alignment between these programs and initial teacher education (Darling-Hammond & Rothman, 2015).

Conclusion

The United States can ameliorate its educational system dramatically if it implements some of the best practices Finland currently uses. Two of these superior methods include an equitable school system and a superior teacher preparation program. Finland had an average educational system before it implemented these two aspects of its system. Ironically, when Finland reformed, it used a few ideas that some Americans believed in many years earlier. Finland's philosophy of education, for example, was identical to John Dewey's. Dewey believed that *all* students were capable of learning decades before Finland reformed its system:

> Comprehensive school reform was not just an organizational change, but a new philosophy of education for Finnish schools. This philosophy included the beliefs that all pupils can learn if they are given proper opportunities and support, that understanding of and learning through human diversity is an important educational goal, and that schools should function as small-scale democracies, just as John Dewey had insisted decades before. (Sahlberg, 2012, pp. 22–23)

One reason Finland's system should attract the attention of American policymakers relates to its relatively moderate levels of expenditure on education. In fact, Finland spends less on education than the United States. This aspect of its system should create hope that the United States can achieve a similar system if it spends its money wisely. In 2011, for example, Finland's total public expenditure on education as a percentage of GDP was 6.5%; however, in the United States, it was 6.9% (Sahlberg, 2015), Such statistics suggest that in creating an outstanding system, spending is less important than efficiency.

Another notable strategy Finland implements relates to its approach toward standardized tests. Because teachers there do not use them to evaluate students, they can focus more on methods that promote creativity and develop high-order thinking skills.

Like any country in the world, Finland faces challenges related to education. Currently, Finland is dealing with a decline in international test scores, vast differences between the academic achievement of boys and girls, and concerns involving teacher induction and professional development programs. It will be interesting to see how this nation deals with these concerns in the near future. Despite these challenges, the superior conditions Finland created to achieve an educational system that outperforms most others deserve attention. These best practices can enhance the American system.

References

Abrams, S. E. (2011, January 27). The children must play. *New Republic*. Retrieved from http://www.newrepublic.com/article/politics/82329/education-reform-Finland-US

Björn, P. M., Aro, M. T., Koponen, T. K., Fuchs, L. S., & Fuchs, D. H. (2016). The many faces of special education within RTI frameworks in the United States and Finland. *Learning Disability Quarterly, 39*(1), 58–66.

Brozo, W. G., & Crain, S. (2016). Schooling in the United States: What we learn from international assessments of reading and math literacy. In H. Morgan & C. Barry (Eds.), *The world leaders in education: Lessons from the successes and drawbacks of their methods* (pp. 37–59). New York, NY: Peter Lang Publishing.

Butler, P. (2016, September 20). No grammar schools, lots of play: The secrets of Europe's top education system. *The Guardian*. Retrieved from https://www.theguardian.com/education/2016/sep/20/grammar-schools-play-europe-top-education-system-finland-daycare

Centers for Disease Control and Prevention. (2010, April). *The association between school-based physical activity, including physical education, and academic performance.* Retrieved from https://www.cdc.gov/healthyyouth/health_and_academics/pdf/pa-pe_paper.pdf

Chenoweth, K. (2009). It can be done, it's being done, and here's how. *Phi Delta Kappan, 91*(1), 38–43.

Conyers, M., & Wilson, D. (2015). Smart moves: Powering up the brain with physical activity. *Phi Delta Kappan, 96*(8), 38–42.

Darling-Hammond, L. (2006). Securing the right to learn: Policy and practice for powerful teaching and learning. *Educational Researcher, 35*(7), 13–24.

Darling-Hammond, L. (2009). *Educational opportunity and alternative certification: New evidence and new questions.* Retrieved from https://edpolicy.stanford.edu/sites/default/files/publications/educational-opportunity-and-alternative-certification-new-evidence-and-new-questions.pdf

Darling-Hammond, L. (2011/2012). Soaring systems. *Education Review, 24*(1), 24–33.

Darling-Hammond, L., & Rothman, R. (2015). *Teaching in the flat world: Learning from high-performing systems.* New York, NY: Teachers College Press.

Dizik, A. (2014, November 3). Does your child really need a tutor? *BBC.* Retrieved from http://www.bbc.com/capital/story/20131016-the-global-tutoring-economy

Donaldson, M. L., & Johnson, S. M. (2011). Teach for America teachers: How long do they teach? Why do they leave? *Phi Delta Kappan, 93*(2), 47–51.

Finnish National Board of Education. (2016). *Compulsory education in Finland.* Retrieved from http://www.oph.fi/download/180148_Compulsory_education_in_Finland.pdf

Heim, J. (2016, December 8). Finland's schools were once the envy of the world. Now, they're slipping. *The Washington Post.* Retrieved from https://www.washingtonpost.com/local/education/finlands-schools-were-once-the-envy-of-the-world-now-theyre-slipping/2016/12/08/dcfd0f56-bd60-11e6-91ee-1adddfe36cbe_story.html?utm_term=.921c54252c49

Kinlan, C. (2011, January 21). Rethinking special education in the U.S. *The Hechinger Report.* Retrieved from http://hechingerreport.org/rethinking-special-education-in-the-u-s/

Kohn, D. (2015, May 16). Let the kids learn through play. *The New York Times.* Retrieved from https://www.nytimes.com/2015/05/17/opinion/sunday/let-the-kids-learn-through-play.html

Lips, D., & Ladner, M. (2009, January 7). How "No Child Left Behind" threatens Florida's successful education reforms. *The Heritage Foundation.* Retrieved from http://www.heritage.org/budget-and-spending/report/how-no-child-left-behind-threatens-floridas-successful-education-reforms

Loveless, T. (2015). Girls, boys, and reading. *The Brookings Institution.* Retrieved from https://www.brookings.edu/research/girls-boys-and-reading/

Organization for Economic Co-operation and Development. (2011). *Strong performers and successful reformers in education: Lessons from PISA for the United States.* Paris: Organization of Economic Cooperation and Development.

Partanen, A. (2011, December 29). What Americans keep ignoring about Finland's school success. *The Atlantic.* Retrieved from https://www.theatlantic.com/national/archive/2011/12/what-americans-keep-ignoring-about-finlands-school-success/250564/

Sahlberg, P. (2011). Lessons from Finland. *American Educator, 35*(2), 34–38.

Sahlberg, P. (2012). A model lesson: Finland shows us what equal opportunity looks like. *American Educator, 36*(1), 20–27.

Sahlberg, P. (2013). Teachers as leaders in Finland. *Educational Leadership, 71*(2), 36–40.

Sahlberg, P. (2015). *Finnish lessons 2.0: What can the world learn from educational change in Finland?* New York, NY: Teachers College Press.

Sarjala, J. (2013). Equality and cooperation: Finland's path to excellence. *American Educator*, *37*(1), 32–36.

Startz, D. (2016, June 20). Teacher pay around the world. *The Brookings Institution*. Retrieved from https://www.brookings.edu/blog/brown-center-chalkboard/2016/06/20/teacher-pay-around-the-world/

Stewart, V. (2012). *A world-class education: Learning from international models of excellence and innovation*. Alexandria, VA: ASCD.

Tucker, M. (2012). Teacher quality: What's wrong with U.S. strategy? *Educational Leadership*, *69*(4), 42–46.

Tucker, M. (2014, February 14). Pasi Sahlberg on Finland's recent PISA results. *Education Week*. Retrieved from http://blogs.edweek.org/edweek/top_performers/2014/02/pasi_sahlberg_on_finlands_recent_pisa_results.html?r=729527101

Välijärvi, J., & Sahlberg, P. (2008). Should "failing" students repeat a grade? Retrospective response from Finland. *Journal of Educational Change*, *9*(4), 385–389.

Wei, R. C., Andree, A., Darling-Hammond, L. (2009). How nations invest in teachers. *Educational Leadership*, *66*(5), 28–33.

Williams, J., & Engel. L. C. (2012). How do other countries evaluate teachers? *Phi Delta Kappan*, *94*(4), 53–57.

FROM A THIRD-WORLD TO A FIRST-WORLD NATION

Education in Singapore Made It Happen

Singapore's educational system deserves notice because in a short time, this nation transformed itself from a poor country to one with a thriving economy in part through the use of outstanding educational practices. These methods created more opportunities for students to receive a high-quality education. The McKinsey Report ranked Singapore highly on its list of best-performing school systems and mentioned that the quality of this country's teachers and instruction are key components of its success (Ministry of Education, 2015). Before exploring how Singapore achieved its high-ranking system, it is worthwhile to explore this country's recent scores in international testing.

In the 21st century, Singapore has consistently ranked among the highest performers in international tests. It surpassed all other countries in all three subjects on the 2015 PISA, with a score of 564 in math, 535 in reading, and 556 in science (Jackson & Kiersz, 2016).

Rapid Progress in a Short Time

With a population of about 5.5 million people, Singapore is a city-state consisting of three major ethnic groups, the Chinese (75%), Malays (13%), and Indians (9%). All citizens and permanent residents can send their children to Singapore's schools, but for holders of temporary visas, entry is on a space-available basis (Sclafani, 2015).

In only 40 years, this country transformed itself from a third-world to a first-world nation. When it gained independence in 1965, it was a poor country with many children who did not go to school. It had a poor-performing education system, little fresh water, poor housing conditions, and repeated conflict among the ethnic groups that resided there. During this time, there was a focus on creating universal primary education as soon as possible (OECD, 2011; Stewart, 2010). Singapore went from an average annual per capita income of $350 in 1965 to an annual per capita income that is over $39,000 today. In 1965, the average person did not go to school after the 3rd grade, but today all students complete at least 10 years of education. Singapore achieved this improvement by enhancing its policies toward preparing, retaining, hiring, assessing, paying, and mentoring its teachers (Sclafani, 2015).

Teacher Preparation

One of the strategies Singapore implemented to enhance its teacher preparation policies included increasing teacher expertise in practical content by decreasing the requirements for courses that were too theoretical, such as those focusing on the philosophy of education. Such an approach allows teachers to be more knowledgeable of relevant fields in the sciences and the humanities. More time is spent on developing practical knowledge like understanding student psychology, thereby allowing teachers to gain the information needed to apply it in the classroom (Tan, 2012).

Only one teacher preparation program offered by the National Institute for Education (NIE) exists in the country. The NIE organizes the teacher education curriculum with the Ministry of Education so that it aligns with the needs of the schools and the expectations of the ministry. Each year the NIE together with the ministry decide on the available openings for teacher trainees at both the elementary and secondary levels. The number of openings is determined by teacher retirements and new programs planned by the ministry. Two paths exist for entering into teacher training: Students can join after completing the 12th grade or after graduating from a college or polytechnic school.

The NIE offers bachelor's and post-graduate degrees. Their programs attract secondary students because pupils do not need to pay tuition, fees, and expenses. They also receive a stipend, worth about half of a first-year teacher's salary. Candidates admitted to the program at the graduate level receive a stipend equivalent to what an employee earns in a civil sector job. Teachers are committed to three years of on-the-job teaching after completing their training. If they fail to provide this service, they must pay back the tuition, stipends, and fees they received.

To be accepted to the teacher preparation programs, students need to be in the top third of their graduating class as measured by grades, national exams, and the teacher entrance proficiency exam. The application process includes interviews designed to determine if the candidates possess the dispositions needed to be good teachers (Sclafani, 2015).

In comparison with the United States, Singapore has much higher standards for entering the teaching profession. Whereas in Singapore teachers are chosen from the top 30% of their graduating class, in the United States, many students planning to enter teacher education programs do so with lower SAT scores than the national average. One method Singapore implemented to attract the best students to the teaching profession included paying them well. Today, the government offers them salaries similar to those the leading professionals in the country earn (Tucker, 2012).

The teacher preparation program provides candidates with strong support and knowledge involving all components of teaching:

> From entry into the teacher preparation program, each teacher candidate receives enormous support to help him or her succeed. The courses deal with all aspects of teaching from content to pedagogy to multicultural issues, student guidance, and character development. Preservice teachers engage in community service in different communities so they can learn about children living in different circumstances. From early in their training, they are in schools to observe, assist, and learn; they do five-week formative and 10-week summative practicums in schools. NIE professors work closely with teachers and administrators in schools to follow the progress of teacher candidates during their practicums. They provide counseling, coaching, and support. (Sclafani, 2015, p. 10)

Teacher Induction

The strong support candidates receive during the teacher preparation program continues as they start their careers. As beginning teachers, they receive support from the school learning community. First-year teachers also have a light workload, about 20% lighter than experienced teachers have, allowing them the time they need to observe other teachers, plan, and chat with their mentor teachers. Furthermore, they receive coaching from department heads, grade-level chairs, and subject-area chairs. These professionals offer more support to those needing it most.

Although there is strong support for novice teachers, a few of them do not perform well or fail to show the professionalism needed to teach. In such cases, the novice teachers may be allowed one more chance at another school, but if they continue to perform poorly, they may be asked to find another profession (Sclafani, 2015).

The strong support first-year teachers receive contributes to Singapore's low attrition rates. In 2016, the *Straits Times* reported that the attrition rate for teachers in Singapore was around 3% (Teng, 2016a). This low attrition rate helps Singapore achieve its success in education. The United States' attrition rate of 8% is considerably higher than Singapore's (Sutcher, Darling-Hammond, & Carver-Thomas, 2016).

High attrition rates can create a plethora of problems that impede student learning and contribute to a chaotic environment. Ronfeldt, Loeb, and Wyckoff (2013), for example, concluded from their study that high teacher turnover rates had a harmful effect on student achievement in both math and English language arts.

Career Options and Support for Improvement

Candidates entering the teaching profession are treated well not only at the start of their careers but at other stages as well. As their careers progress, they have options to choose from regarding various paths they can take that match their aspirations. The Education Service Professional Development and Career Plan (Edu-Pac) helps teachers achieve their aspirations and includes three components: a career path, recognition through monetary rewards, and an evaluation system. Teachers can pursue three tracks: a teaching track, a leadership track, or a specialist track.

If they choose the teaching track, teachers continue to work in the classroom and advance to the level of master teacher. Those who pursue the leadership track assume leadership positions in schools and in the Ministry of Education. The specialist track permits teachers to work for the Ministry of Education as specialists with deep knowledge, allowing them to contribute to Singapore's superior approach to education (OECD, 2013a).

Part of Edu-Pac is a system called the Enhanced Performance Management System (EPMS), which supports teacher improvement and performance. This system describes the skills, knowledge, and professional characteristics for each track. EPMS is a competency-based system involving coaching, evaluation, and performance planning:

> In performance planning, the teacher starts the year with a self-assessment and develops goals for teaching, instructional innovations and improvements at the school, professional development, and personal development. The teacher meets with his/her reporting officer, who is usually the head of a department, for a discussion about setting targets and performance benchmarks. Performance coaching takes place throughout the year, particularly during the formal mid-year review, when the reporting officer meets with the teacher to discuss progress and needs. In the performance evaluation held at the end of the year, the reporting officer conducts the appraisal interview and reviews actual performance against planned performance. The performance grade given influences the annual performance bonus received for the year's work. During the performance evaluation phase, decisions regarding promotions to the next level are made based on "current estimated potential" (CEP). The decision about a teacher's current CEP is made in consultation with senior staff who have worked with the teacher, and is based on observations, discussions with the teacher, evidence of portfolio, and knowledge of the teacher's contribution to the school and community. (OECD, 2013a, p. 69)

School Structure

In addition to the outstanding methods used to support teacher improvement are other components of Singapore's schools system that shed light on why this country achieved its success in education. Some of these features involve the structure of its school system and the country's policies on bilingual education, special education, and compulsory education.

Although school instruction in Singapore is in English, all students need to learn the mother tongue language. The mother tongue languages are Chinese, Malay, and Tamil. The ministry implements such a policy to provide students with the skills to develop a global outlook and to communicate well with Asian cultures. This approach also aids students to appreciate and gain more awareness of their own culture.

Although mainstream schools in Singapore have the resources to teach students with mild special educational needs, those with severe disabilities go to different schools. The ministry funds 20 of these schools. Each school has its own curriculum, pedagogy, and special services that are customized according to student needs. The purpose of these schools is to develop the skills and values students need to live fulfilling lives. The ministry has worked with these schools, providing the guidance they need to offer effective education (Ministry of Education, 2015).

Compulsory education was mandated in Singapore in 2003. The Compulsory Education Act defines compulsory school age as the age above six years and under the age of 15, requiring any child in this age group to attend a national school unless exempted. Students exempted can be receiving special education, attending a designated school, or getting instruction at home. Only a small percentage of students are not enrolled in national schools. If children fail to attend school without an exemption, their parents or guardians could be charged with an offense involving a fine not exceeding $5,000, imprisonment for a period not exceeding 12 months, or both (Ministry of Education, 2017).

Preschool Education

Before attending the compulsory school system, most children attend preschool. In 2010, for example, only 1.1% of six-year-old children did not attend preschool (Lim-Ratnam, 2013). The Ministry of Education's philosophy is that the early years are critical for children and that preschool programs should offer children chances to build self-confidence and social skills. These components of development are crucial for building a strong foundation for future success. One of the ministry's goals is to provide high-quality preschool education that is affordable to Singaporeans. Another goal involves providing guidance on teaching practices and learning resources that can be shared with the preschool sector. Currently, 15 Ministry of Education Kindergartens exist in Singapore. They are located within primary schools and community spaces and designed to encourage collaboration (Ministry of Education, 2016a).

To enhance kindergarten education in Singapore, the ministry created the Nurturing Early Learners Curriculum. This resource provides tools to help early childhood educators grow professionally and expand their knowledge and confidence. The ministry also collaborated with the Early Childhood Development Agency to train educators to implement this curriculum effectively (Ministry of Education, 2015).

Primary and Secondary Education

Singapore's school system is based on six years of primary education and four to five years of secondary education. During the primary years, students go through four years of foundational instruction that focuses on English, mathematics, and mother tongue language. Moral education, social studies, art, music, and physical education are also taught. In 2008, subject-based banding superseded streaming (OECD, 2014).

Subject-based banding is believed to offer more flexibility for students because it allows them to select a combination of standard and foundation subjects depending on their academic level. If a child is weak in math, for example, the student can choose to take this subject at the foundation level but take others at the standard level. Implementing this approach allows teachers to provide support for students who are weak in certain areas while expanding their knowledge of the disciplines they excel in. Schools identify students' weak subjects through examinations. Then, they recommend a combination of subject levels based on exam results (Ministry of Education, 2016b). Over 95% of students in Singapore attend schools that group students by ability across classes (OECD, 2013b).

After students complete the sixth grade, they take the Primary School Leaving Examination in English, mathematics, mother tongue language, and science. The results of this test determine which type of school they will go to. The different kinds of schools include express, normal academic, or normal technical. Students admitted to the express schools enter a four-year program that ends with the general certificate of education at the (GCE) O-level. Those going to normal academic schools enter a four-year program at the GCE N-level; however, they may take the O-level exam in year five. Those in the normal technical schools follow a four-year program at the GCE-N level that prepares them for the Institute for Technical Education and technical higher education (OECD, 2014).

Although students are admitted to a particular type of school, the system is flexible, allowing for lateral transfers and opportunities for students to take more challenging courses. In addition to taking academic courses, students at the secondary level can enroll in art and music programs. These programs encourage students to grow holistically and allow pupils to further develop their talent in and love for these activities. Students at this level also participate in physical activities and sports.

Other types of schools are available for students with unique needs. For example, some schools, referred to as "specialized schools," offer hands-on and practical programs. Other types of schools, known as "specialized independent schools," offer students the chance to pursue mathematics, sciences, sports, and the arts at a higher level. Some schools offer an "integrated program," a six-year program for students who prefer a less-structured learning style. This program engages students with strong academic skills and a desire to pursue nonacademic topics through broader learning experiences (Ministry of Education, 2016c).

Superior Social Policies

In addition to flexible programs, Singapore practices methods that promote equity not only in education but also in other aspects of its society. Ever since the country gained independence, the government has made an effort to prevent the kind of elitist society that existed previously. This effort has led to the meritocratic society that constitutes Singapore today, a society with a strong commitment to equity where talent and hard work are rewarded.

When the country first gained independence, achievement gaps between the Chinese population and the other cultural groups existed; however, as a result of the newly implemented policies, these gaps have been reduced considerably. One policy previously practiced was streaming. While this method was contentious, it was effective in reducing dropout rates. Another policy designed to aid families in need was created, providing them with financial help. In addition, Singapore's housing policies are believed to reduce academic achievement gaps between different groups because 80% of the people reside in housing built by the government with a deliberate mix of ethnic groups on each block. These policies lead to more chances for children to be in a community with high expectations. Such strategies have helped Singapore improve not only its achievement gaps but also its graduation rates. Today, the country has a secondary school graduation rate of 98% (OECD, 2014; Stewart, 2011).

As previously discussed, Singapore allows chances for students to move horizontally between streams at the secondary level. The country is also known for the resources and attention it provides to struggling students. For example, Singapore identifies struggling readers through a screening test starting in the first grade and then provides them with support programs, assigning teachers to work with them in groups of 8–10 students. Similar support is available in mathematics. Low-income students receive support at the early childhood level because the government provides funds to preschools that cater for these students. The country also provides tremendous resources to its vocational and technical training programs, leading it to develop a reputation as one of the best in the world in this arena (OECD, 2014; Stewart, 2011).

These strategies exemplify Singapore's commitment to offering various ways for diverse students to succeed and show why this nation has a higher percentage of low-income students that succeed academically than many other countries. An OECD (2013c) report indicated that over half of students in Singapore came from a disadvantaged socioeconomic background but performed much better than would be predicted by their background. This percentage is well over the OECD average. In the United States, on the other hand, the percentage of these students is well below the OECD average.

The Classroom Environment

Different opinions exist on the ways teachers provide instruction in Singapore. One perspective is based on the idea that teachers there do not integrate a sustained approach for developing higher-order thinking and interdisciplinary learning. Instead, this view supports the notion that teachers focus on curricular content delivery and examination performance and apply this style of teaching as a result of their views about education. According to Deng and Gopinathan (2016), for example, teachers in Singapore tend to believe that knowledge consists of facts contained in the national curriculum and in textbooks and that students need to master it through instruction designed to enhance performance on examinations. Consequently, teachers frequently regard teaching as transmitting knowledge in the curriculum and view learning as mastering this knowledge through memorization and practice.

Although various reform initiatives promoted the use of innovative approaches of pedagogical practice, critics of Singapore's school system say that its teaching methods have to a great extent remained traditional and lack an emphasis on developing higher-order thinking. Such critics say that the dominant method of teaching involves whole-class lectures that include time for question-and-answer sequences. This style emphasizes assigning worksheets and homework so that students can master specific procedures and problem-solving skills (Deng & Gopinathan, 2016).

This perspective is justifiable because the meritocratic national examination system in Singapore provides students who do well on their exams more educational and career opportunities than those who do not. Because high scores on examinations are strongly linked to educational and career success in Asian nations, it is easy to see how teachers can be more inclined to teach to examinations rather than experiment with innovative methods of teaching and learning.

A different perspective on education in Singapore supports the idea that Singapore's reputation as a place with rote-oriented schools is exaggerated. This view expresses that the initiatives implemented to enhance the school system have worked to a great degree. Linda Darling-Hammond (2010), for example, wrote the following about the vision to change Singapore's schools so that students rely less on rote learning and more on innovative teaching methods:

> When visiting schools in Singapore, I was struck by how much this vision has been actualized through the highly connected work of the ministry; its major partner for professional preparation, the National Institute for Education, and the school sites. At every school, an emphasis on holistic education to develop well-rounded human beings was apparent. Explicit effort to develop students cognitively, aesthetically, spiritually, morally, and socially were obvious throughout the curriculum. In addition to project work visible in nearly every classroom, children were extensively involved in music, arts, calligraphy, physical education, sports, and an amazing variety of clubs and self-initiated activities aimed at building creativity and entrepreneurship. (p. 186)

Historical Background

To better understand how Singapore created a system that promotes equity and how it achieved its success in education, it is important to explore the country from a historical perspective starting with the years when it gained independence. The country's first effort to create an effective school system was unsuccessful.

During the time it gained independence, Singapore endured high unemployment rates and high population growth. The nation concentrated on quickly expanding basic education by unifying schools created by different ethnic groups into one system. In 1965, Singapore created universal primary education, followed by universal lower secondary education in the early 1970s. Although it had created a national system of public education during this period, it was a poor school system with a high dropout rate that failed to create a work force capable of competing with other Asian nations. A new approach was needed (OECD, 2011; Stewart, 2011).

The First Reforms

The first set of reforms started in 1979. One of the goals at this time was to lower the dropout rate by increasing vocational education and creating more ways for students to succeed. Rather than educate all students in one type of school, the new approach emphasized various pathways. The new way included the use of academic high schools designed to prepare students for college; polytechnic high schools designed for technical training as well as college preparation; and technical institutes designed for technical training but for lower-level students.

Schools also began to track students starting in the elementary grades. This controversial practice of separating students based on ability was unpopular; however, the new set of reforms worked as dropout rates declined significantly by 1986. In addition, many more students passed the O-level English examinations. Sixteen years after the reforms were implemented, Singapore was number one in the world on the TIMSS in math and science (OECD, 2011; Stewart, 2011).

The "Thinking Schools, Learning Nation" Initiative

In the late 1980s, the Ministry of Education recognized that the school system overemphasized examination performance and that a broader educational approach was needed. Although the creation of multiple pathways for students to continue their education alleviated this concern, a new plan that included a different way for dealing with this problem was implemented in 1997 (Deng & Gopinathan, 2016).

The "thinking schools, learning nation" initiative called for integrating technology in every school and emphasized intellectual curiosity and creative thinking. For this approach to be applied effectively, teachers would need to focus more on project-based and independent learning. Consequently, the amount of content they were required to cover was reduced by 10 to 30% in 1998 (Darling-Hammond, 2010).

The idea of "teach less, learn more" became a popular slogan in 2004 when Prime Minister Lee Hsien Loong used these words during a speech to urge for a teaching style that encourages teachers to cover less material in order to increase student initiative and depth of study. Although previous reforms had improved education, children were still believed to be too passive. During the speech, the prime minister mentioned that the school system should not increase the syllabus or assign more homework. He said that the new approach would lead to less pressure on students and less rote learning, but they would have more chances to discover and explore. The prime minister also urged parents to support the efforts of this approach rather than complain about the decrease in work (Government of Singapore, 2004).

Areas Needing Improvement

Although scholars hold different views about the extent to which the education reforms have enhanced the teaching and learning environment in Singaporean schools, there is evidence indicating that education in Singapore often promotes rote learning as a result of the importance placed on exams. Because preparing students for exams leads to lower-level thinking skills and a lack of creativity, this area needs improvement.

Rote-Learning Methods

The many hours students receive tutoring contribute to rote learning and to inequalities as well. Most students (97%) in Singapore receive tutoring. Although the country provides methods that promote equity, tutoring contributes to inequalities because wealthier families can afford better tutors (Gooch, 2012). In addition, the extra hours students spend with tutors are often used for drills that will help pupils score highly on exams rather than for project-based learning. Local bookstores reflect this trend and contain large quantities of assessment manuals that include sample questions of content from the school curriculum (Nayak, 2016).

Although school reforms were designed to add new methods to help students discover and explore rather than learn through memorization, Singaporean students still rely on rote drills to do well on exams. For example, a father of a nine-year-old described a math word problem and the strategies students are taught to solve such problems. He mentioned that the reason Singaporean students are so good at math does not involve superior intelligence but the drills they do that allow them to answer questions with limited thinking skills:

The reason is not superior intelligence; it is simply because kids here are drilled on similar types of problems using model drawing. This method cuts short the actual thinking required for such types of questions and provides quick, almost effortless, solutions that can be regurgitated in exams.

There is, however, one big caveat: Children can solve such questions in exams only if they have solved them before. It is virtually impossible for even the most mathematically-inclined child to develop an original solution for a new problem in a time-constrained exam setting. (Jayaraman, 2017, paras. 12–13)

High Stress Levels

The importance of exams in Singapore also leads to unbearable stress levels for some students that can lead to suicide. This process starts at a young age when parents set up activities for their children that encourage the use of books rather than play. Unfortunately, some parents put too much pressure on their children. For example, when one mother reprimanded her 13-year-old girl for carelessly answering one question, the child received a referral to a clinic for treatment for anxiety, self-harm, and depression. Another mother insisted that her son take the Primary School Leaving Examination for a second time, even after he passed it the first time (Teng, 2016b).

The concerns over the stress levels related to academic achievement increased in 2016 when the death of an 11-year-old boy was determined to be a suicide. On the day he was to reveal his mid-year examination results to his parents, he fell 17 floors from his bedroom window. A state official reacted by reminding parents that children may study, but their effort is not always reflected in test results. He also emphasized that poor performance is frequently temporary and that parents ought to regularly remind their children that the family will always provide support even in difficult situations involving children's academic performance.

The victim of the suicide received a kite after telling his mother he got average results on his exam papers as he had in previous years. However, his scores were well below what his mother expected. A few days later, his mother noticed that he was not wearing the appropriate attire for school, so she asked him to change into the right clothes. The boy then went into his room and locked the door. When his parents discovered the door locked, they found a spare key and opened the door only to discover that he had jumped out of the window (Hussain, 2016).

In response to the stress placed on students to do well on exams, changes will be made to reduce the overemphasis on exam scores. For example, there will no longer be an aggregate score on the national examination in 2021, and children will no longer be graded relative to one another. More emphasis is already being placed on encouraging pupils to express themselves and developing their character and life skills. In the near future, children will have increased opportunities to attend secondary schools that provide more programs in robotics, environmental issues, the arts, music, drama, and dance to develop their interests in more areas.

While these changes provide hope for a better environment for students to develop, it is not clear whether parents will change their attitudes toward education. Performing well on the Primary School Leaving Examination is an obsession in Singapore. Although changes are made to reduce stress, some parents still aim to invest in the shadow education industry, which has expanded considerably since 2004. They spend thousands of dollars each month, hoping their children will enter a good secondary school (Teng & Yang, 2016).

Conclusion

Many aspects of the Singaporean school system would enhance the systems of other nations. Some of the most important practices this nation implements include those that create opportunities for the poor to learn. In Singapore, 20% of the most disadvantaged 15-year-olds outperform 10% of the most privileged students in the United States. Such an accomplishment occurs as the result of outstanding strategies that include attracting highly qualified teachers to serve the neediest students (Tan, 2016).

Another impressive characteristic of this system relates to its expenditure on education. Singapore spends less per student than most OECD countries. In 2012, for example, it spent 3.1% of its GDP on education, less than the OECD average of 5.3%. The country produces highly educated students by spending less than many countries because its methods are efficient. For example, rather than hire many unskilled teachers to work with small groups of students, Singaporean educational leaders believe that it is better to use fewer highly qualified teachers to teach large groups. Consequently, classes there are large. In primary school, for example, the average number of students is 35.5, well above the OECD average of 24.1 pupils per class (Tan, 2016).

While other nations can borrow such strategies with success, other aspects of Singapore's academic success may be more difficult to implement abroad. One of these aspects relates to student attitudes toward education. Like some of the other Asian nations discussed in this book, students in Singapore tend to believe that hard work is the reason for academic success rather than inherited intelligence. In many countries, students blame their teacher for poor academic performance, but in Singapore students tend to trust their teachers and believe they will succeed if they work hard (Tan, 2016).

Although it may be difficult to implement certain aspects of education that originate abroad, the idea of borrowing practices from other nations is feasible. In fact, Singapore modeled some of their methods on theories and research originating in other countries. For example, some of their textbooks were designed according to the theories of Jerome Bruner. Bruner maintained that learning occurs by first using real objects, then images, and then symbols. Singapore used this theory to develop their approach to teaching math. This approach focuses on implementing visual aids to model math problems and using blocks to represent fractions or ratios. As a result of covering a narrower curriculum than those of many nations and using superior approaches of teaching, students in Singapore usually learn fewer concepts but cover them in greater depth (Vasagar, 2016).

Unfortunately, debate exists about the level at which Singaporean students learn. Although they may be able to score highly on tests that require problem-solving skills like the PISA, they may not be as creative or innovative as students in other countries. The reason for this outcome involves the many hours of tutoring they receive and the emphasis placed on exams that promote learning through rote methods, thereby not allowing students to experiment or think in new ways. Additionally, the stress placed on students to do well on exams contributes to unhealthy child development.

In response to these concerns, new ways of teaching have been introduced. Students at the early primary level no longer have to take exams, and in the future, primary school graduates will have more options regarding the secondary schools they can attend. To reduce pressure on students, the practice of naming the highest scorer on the Primary School Leaving Examination ended in 2012. One year later, the ministry ended revealing the lowest and highest scores. The new way of recognizing students who perform well and those who improve involves acknowledging their achievements in groups rather than individually. The ministry also introduced a physical education syllabus in 2014, allowing 10 to 20% of time in schools to be used for outdoor education (Teng & Yang, 2016).

It is difficult, however, to predict the extent to which such changes will alleviate the concerns associated with the Singaporean school system because parents in this country have strong attitudes about education. They send their children to tutors frequently and hold high academic expectations as a result of what is sometimes described as an obsession with education. Although schools may promote more innovative strategies and ways to develop students holistically, the pressure cooker atmosphere may continue for many students.

References

Darling-Hammond, L. (2010). *The flat world and education: How America's commitment to equity will determine our future.* New York, NY: Teachers College Press.

Deng, Z., & Gopinathan, S. (2016). PISA and high-performing education systems: Explaining Singapore's education success. *Comparative Education, 52*(4), 449–472.

Gooch, L. (2012, August 12). Tutoring spreads beyond Asia's wealthy. *The New York Times.* Retrieved from http://www.nytimes.com/2012/08/06/world/asia/06iht-educlede06.html

Government of Singapore. (2004). *Prime Minister Lee Hsien Loong's National Day Rally 2004.* Retrieved from http://www.pmo.gov.sg/newsroom/prime-minister-lee-hsien-loongs-national-day-rally-2004-english

Hussain, A. (2016, October 21). Death of boy, 11, who fell 17 floors after failing his exams for the first time ruled a suicide. *The Straits Times.* Retrieved from http://www.straitstimes.com/singapore/courts-crime/death-of-boy-11-who-fell-17-floors-after-failing-his-exams-for-the-first-time

Jackson, A., & Kiersz, A. (2016, December 6). The latest ranking of top countries in math, reading, and science is out—and the US didn't crack the top 10. *Business Insider.* Retrieved from http://www.businessinsider.com/pisa-worldwide-ranking-of-math-science-reading-skills-2016-12

Jayaraman, B. (2017, February 17). Let's kill the drill approach in schools. *The Straits Times.* Retrieved from http://www.straitstimes.com/opinion/lets-kill-the-drill-approach-in-schools

Lim-Ratnam, C. (2013). Tensions in defining quality pre-school education: The Singapore context. *Educational Review, 65*(4), 416–431.

Ministry of Education. (2015). *Bringing out the best in every child.* Retrieved from https://www.moe.gov.sg/docs/default-source/document/about/files/moe-corporate-brochure.pdf

Ministry of Education. (2016a). *Pre-school: A strong start foe every child.* Retrieved from https://www.moe.gov.sg/education/preschool

Ministry of Education. (2016b). *Subject-based banding: Catering to your child's abilities.* Retrieved from https://www.moe.gov.sg/education/primary/subject-based-banding

Ministry of Education. (2016c). *Education statistics digest 2016: Moulding the future of our nation.* Retrieved from https://www.moe.gov.sg/docs/default-source/document/publications/education-statistics-digest/esd-2016.pdf

Ministry of Education. (2017). *Compulsory education.* Retrieved from https://www.moe.gov.sg/education/education-system/compulsory-education#footnote-1

Nayak, S. (2016, January 5). Singapore schools: "The best education system in the world" putting significant stress on young children. *Australian Broadcasting Corporation*. Retrieved from http://www.abc.net.au/news/2016-01-06/best-education-system-putting-stress-on-singaporean-children/6831964

Organization for Economic Co-operation and Development. (2011). *Strong performers and successful reformers in education: Lessons from PISA for the United States*. Paris: Organization of Economic Cooperation and Development.

Organization for Economic Co-operation and Development. (2013a). *Teachers for the 21ˢᵗ century: Using evaluation to improve teaching*. Paris: Organization of Economic Cooperation and Development.

Organization for Economic Co-operation and Development. (2013b). *PISA 2012 results: What makes schools successful? Resources, policies and practices (Volume IV)*. Paris: Organization of Economic Cooperation and Development.

Organization for Economic Co-operation and Development. (2013c). *PISA 2012 results: Excellence through equity: Giving every student the chance to succeed (Volume II)*. Paris: Organization of Economic Cooperation and Development.

Organization for Economic Co-operation and Development. (2014). *Strong performers and successful reformers in education: Lessons from PISA for Korea*. Paris: Organization of Economic Cooperation and Development.

Ronfeldt, M., Loeb, S., & Wyckoff, J. (2013). How teacher turnover harms student achievement. *American Educational Research Journal, 50*(1), 4–36.

Sclafani, S. K. (2015). Singapore chooses teachers carefully. *Phi Delta Kappan, 97*(3), 8–13.

Stewart, V. (2010). Singapore leads the way in changing teacher education. *Phi Delta Kappan, 92*(2), 92–93.

Stewart, V. (2011). Singapore: A journey to the top, step by step. In M. Tucker (Ed.), *Surpassing Shanghai: An agenda for American education built on the world's leading systems* (pp. 113–139). Cambridge, MA: Harvard Education Press.

Sutcher, L., Darling-Hammond, L., & Carver-Thomas, D. (2016). A coming crisis in teaching? Teacher supply, demand, and shortages in the U.S. *Learning Policy Institute*. Retrieved from https://learningpolicyinstitute.org/product/coming-crisis-teaching

Tan, J. (2016, September 7). Singapore debunks myths about western education. *The National*. Retrieved from http://www.thenational.ae/world/southeast-asia/singapore-debunks-myths-about-western-education

Tan, O. S. (2012). Singapore's holistic approach to teacher development. *Phi Delta Kappan, 94*(3), 76–77.

Teng, A. (2016a, October 23). Helping teachers to manage their workload. *The Straits Times*. Retrieved from http://www.straitstimes.com/singapore/education/helping-teachers-to-manage-their-workload

Teng, A. (2016b, October 30). Exam stress among the young: When grades define worth. *The Straits Times*. Retrieved from http://www.straitstimes.com/singapore/when-grades-define-worth

Teng, A., & Yang, C. (2016, April 17). Going beyond grades: Evolving the Singapore education system. *The Straits Times*. Retrieved from http://www.straitstimes.com/singapore/education/going-beyond-grades-evolving-the-singapore-education-system

Tucker, M. (2012). Teacher quality: What's wrong with U.S. strategy? *Educational Leadership*, 69(4), 42–46.

Vasagar, J. (2016, July 22). Why Singapore's kids are so good at maths. *Financial Times*. Retrieved from https://www.ft.com/content/2e4c61f2-4ec8-11e6-8172-e39ecd3b86fc

· 4 ·

JAPAN

Always on Top in Education

Unlike some of the other countries covered in this book, Japan participated in the first international assessment ever offered. This test, called the First International Mathematics Study (FIMS), was implemented in 1964. Only 12 countries participated at that time. Unlike the United States, which also participated, Japan did well on this assessment and has continued its impressive performance on each subsequent international assessment measuring the academic ability of its students. On the 2015 PISA, for example, students in Japan ranked 2nd in science, 5th in math, and 8th in reading (Aoki, 2016).

Those who interact with young Japanese people often rave about their intelligence:

> Some seasoned observers report that average Japanese high school graduates who enter colleges compare favorably in terms of what they know and can do to average American college graduates. Less generous observers report that they compare to American college students with two years of college. Other observers note that many Japanese high school graduates know more about the geography and history of many other countries than do natives of those countries. (Tucker & Ruzzi, 2011, p. 79)

How does Japan regularly keep producing highly educated people and achieving impressive scores on international tests? One reason has to do with the way teachers are selected. Like some other high-ranking nations in education,

Japan scrutinizes its teacher candidates and selects only those with the best credentials. Teacher candidates must pass an exam offered by a prefecture, a region with a board of education similar to a county in the United States. These exams are difficult. In 2014, for example, only 14% of teacher applicants who applied for a junior high school position passed their initial exam (Ahn, Asanuma, & Mori, 2016).

Strong Support for Beginning Teachers

In addition to going through a rigorous selection process, beginning teachers in Japan receive strong support that contributes to the country's high retention rate for new teachers. Only 1.35% of Japan's beginning teachers left the profession after their first year in 2006, a remarkable percentage considering that in the United States almost one-third of teachers leave after their first three years (Ahn, 2014). The low levels of cohesion among teachers in countries with high turnover rates hamper student achievement and teaching effectiveness. What is also remarkable about Japan's high teacher retention rates involves the many more hours they work in comparison with American teachers. In fact, lower secondary teachers in Japan average 53.9 hours of work per week, the highest number among OECD member countries. Many teachers in Japan stay at school until 7 p.m. or later. Sometimes, they even come in on weekends to fulfill additional responsibilities, such as attending meetings, providing student guidance, and preparing reports (Ahn, 2016).

Each prefecture takes the appropriate steps for new teachers to develop the skills needed to do well, assuming their new employees have the intelligence to succeed but not necessarily the job skills to perform well. Thus, the prefectures provide induction programs that allow new teachers ample time (one entire year) to apprentice with experienced master teachers. During this time, the master teachers are exempt from their normal teaching routine so that they can work with the apprentices (OECD, 2011).

The induction program requires first-year teachers to participate in structured and unstructured professional development opportunities, requiring them to complete 10 hours of on-site training each week and 25 days of training off-site. Although the professional development programs may benefit new teachers, they sometimes do not address many of their immediate needs (Ahn et al., 2016).

Another component of the Japanese educational system that plays a crucial role in maintaining Japan's high retention rate is the teacher's room or *shokuin shitsu*, a place in the school where all teachers collaborate with each other every day. The teacher's room reflects the Japanese cultural belief of valuing the group over the individual and promotes a nurturing environment for new teachers as they get guidance from more experienced professionals. Senior teachers also view videotapes of new teachers' teaching and offer feedback, and rather than fire beginning teachers who perform poorly, Japan retrains them (Hatton, 2010).

The Japanese believe that it is crucial to contribute to the group because the group will respond back to help the individual, but if someone shuns the group, the group will not help this person succeed (Tucker & Ruzzi, 2011). As a result of these values, teachers in Japan frequently interact with other teachers in the teacher's room and provide strong support for new teachers (Ahn, 2014, 2016).

High Levels of Collaboration

Another example of the strong collaboration among teachers involves how they design lessons. Rather than design them individually, they work in groups. After a plan is completed, one teacher teaches the lesson to a class as the others observe. The group then meets to assess the teacher's performance, offering suggestions for improvement. Other schools can send their teachers to observe and participate in the evaluation. This process leads to a superior method of accountability:

> This practice is entirely consistent with the way teams work in private industry. It also reflects the Japanese focus on relying on groups to get work done. But it has a profound impact on the practice of teaching. Indeed, it is the best hope for the continual, sustained improvement of teaching practice. It brings the work of teaching out from behind the closed door of the classroom and the individual teacher and opens it up for inspection and critique by colleagues. There is very strong teacher accountability in Japan, not in the form of formalised accountability to the bureaucracy, but instead an intimate and very real accountability to one's colleagues. Because they do not want to let the group down, teachers work hard to develop superior lesson plans, to teach them well, and to provide sound and useful critiques when it is their colleague's turn to demonstrate their lesson plans to them. (OECD, 2011, p. 145)

Whereas in the United States policies such as RttP rewarded individual teachers if their students performed well on exams, in Japan more emphasis is placed on group evaluations rather than on individual teacher evaluations. The Japanese believe that the work of many teachers rather than just one enables students to excel. Thus, evaluating groups of teachers rather than individual teachers is believed to lead to cohesion, the sharing of best practices, and a high level of collaboration. The collaboration among teachers in Japan sometimes involves teachers who travel from across the country to participate in public lessons. In previous years, this cooperation occurred when the subject of solar cells was added to the science curriculum. Thousands of researchers and teachers participated in public lessons, leading to valuable information about the practical ways to teach this topic (Stewart, 2012).

Unlike the high level of collaboration in Japan, in the United States, teachers usually work alone most of the school day. They use only about 3% of their time in school working with colleagues according to a study by Scholastic and the Gates Foundation (Mirel & Goldin, 2012).

Special Education in Japan

The strong cohesion among teachers in Japan helps students with special needs succeed. Japan does not hold back struggling students because many of them get the help they need. When teachers meet, they discuss the learning problems of their students and respond by providing individual attention to these pupils. Students performing poorly in certain subjects often get additional instruction after school (OECD, 2011).

The traditional way of educating Japanese children with disabilities has been to place them in special schools. In the 1980s, however, organizations representing disabled people expressed a preference for mainstream schooling, leading to a gradual increase in the number of these students in mainstream schools. In 2006, reforms occurred that encouraged these students to attend mainstream schools (Mithout, 2016).

Today, many students in Japan with special needs attend heterogeneous regular classrooms. The Japanese believe that success is achieved through hard work. Through hard work and the additional guidance they receive from their teachers, struggling students succeed frequently and proceed to the next grade. For pupils who need special schools because it is impossible for them to learn in the same way students in traditional schools learn, such schools exist. In addition, some students attend special classes at traditional schools. As a result of this approach to education, Japan places about half as many of their students in special education programs as some Western countries do (OECD, 2011; Tucker & Ruzzi, 2011).

More Hours of Study

In addition to the advantages of a collaborative teaching environment, Japanese students excel academically simply because they spend more hours studying. In contrast to students in Finland, who are assigned a small amount of homework, Japanese children have several hours to do per day. They also have a shorter summer vacation than many of their counterparts in other nations—only six weeks (OECD, 2011).

For many years, students in Japan went to school for six days a week, but the Ministry of Education, Culture, Sports, Science, and Technology (MEXT) implemented a nationwide policy early in the 21st century to limit this number of days from six to five. Despite the attempt to reduce stress on students, many schools in Tokyo continued to hold classes on Saturday because the policy allowed for classes to be held on a sixth day if there were "special needs." Some schools in Tokyo used this loophole to justify having classes on Saturdays (Baines & Yasuda, 2016).

Many students receive instruction after school in private cram schools that help struggling students and provide advanced study for those who have mastered school content. A recent study indicated that about 15.9% of elementary school children in Japan go to cram schools and that this percentage increases to approximately 62.5% when they reach their third year of junior high school (Lowe, 2015). The cram school industry is a big business with over 50,000 cram schools in Japan. Parents often pay large sums of money to send their children to these schools. In 2010, for example, families spent 924 billion yen (US$12 billion) on private tutoring (Allen, 2016).

Today, newer types of classes offering individualized instruction have increased. Traditional cram schools consist of big classes with many students; however, the pace is sometimes too fast for some students, thereby frustrating those who need more guidance. Although parents pay more for smaller classes (about 40,000 yen or $400 a month) than what they would pay for a traditional class, students in such classes tend to learn more. Some of these classes consist of one teacher and one student, while others consist of one teacher with a small group of students (Nagano, 2014).

Carefully Designed Instruction

The more hours students spend on academic work and the strong collaboration among teachers are not the only factors that lead to the academic success of Japanese students. Teachers in Japan know how to engage students and teach in a manner that promotes critical thinking. Although Japanese students may memorize information when studying for their college entrance exams, teachers do not use a style of instruction that promotes lower-level thinking skills. In fact, Japanese teachers usually use methods that encourage students to learn content at a higher level of depth than the level at which many students in American schools learn. They integrate collaborative learning activities and hands-on supports in a way that requires students to apply knowledge. The exaggerated views some Americans have of Asian schools as places that promote memorization without developing critical thinking skills were debunked by Harold Stevenson's and James Stigler's research in the early 1990s (Darling-Hammond, 2010).

The strong collaboration among teachers leads to lessons that are organized and highly engaging. To illustrate this way of teaching, Harold Stevenson and James Stigler (1992) observed a fifth-grade math class in Japan and described how a teacher got her students' attention by walking in a class with a bag filled with clinking glass.

The teacher then took a beer bottle, a vase, and a pitcher out of the bag and asked the students which one would hold the most water. The students concurred that to find the answer, they needed to fill the containers with water. Later in the lesson, the students were divided into groups to measure how many cups they needed to fill the container that the teacher gave them. When the students were done, the teacher showed the class the results in the form of a bar graph and then ended the class with a review of what they had learned. The teacher started and continued the lesson without going over concepts and definitions, and she only mentioned a few terms about graphs at the very end of the class. Elementary math lessons in Japan therefore tend to focus on problem solving rather than rote mastery of facts.

Teacher Preparation Programs

The engaging lessons teachers provide in Japan are much more likely to result from what they learn after they complete their teacher preparation programs rather than from what they learn while in these programs. In fact, Americans may be surprised to learn that university teacher preparation programs in Japan require only four weeks of clinical experience, a much shorter period than the one semester to one year required in the United States. Finland has an even higher one-year minimum. Japanese teacher candidates do not need as much time in their university clinical experiences as their counterparts in other countries because when they first get hired, they experience tremendous support and work in a highly collaborative environment (Ahn, 2014).

To get a teaching certificate, candidates need to complete a teacher preparation program accredited by the Ministry of Education. Teacher certificates are offered at three levels—advanced, first level, and second level. In order to get an advanced level certificate, a candidate needs to have a master's degree or higher. The first level certificate is for a candidate with a bachelor's degree. Individuals with junior college degrees earn the second level certificate, a temporary certificate that expires after 15 years. Additionally, three kinds of certificates are offered. Elementary teachers can get a general certificate, which is a non-subject-specific certificate, or a "special-subject certificate" for teaching topics such as music and art. Secondary school teachers are required to have a "subject-based certificate" (Fujita & Dawson, 2007).

Organization of the Educational System and the Schools

In both the public and private sectors, MEXT monitors all components of education. The academic year runs from April to March and consists of trimesters: April to mid-July, September to late December, and January to late March. Like most American universities, colleges and universities in Japan operate with a two-term semester system that runs from April to September and October to March.

The Japanese educational system works on a structure introduced in 1947 when the Fundamental Law of Education was passed. This structure is based on six years of elementary education, three years of lower secondary school, three years of upper secondary school, and four years at a university. Both primary and lower secondary education are compulsory, but upper secondary school is not (Clark, 2005).

Japan spends little on public education compared with other countries. Indeed, among the OECD countries providing data in 2012, Japan shared a spot with Slovakia for spending the least amount on public education as a percentage of GDP according to the *Japan Times* (Otake, 2015). One of the ways school costs are cut is by having students clean their classroom rather than hiring janitors. In addition to learning academic content, Japanese students learn how to behave like good citizens and to take responsibility for their actions. A few American schools have experimented with this approach as well (Philips, 2015). The Japanese also cut costs by spending less on school buildings, full color glossy textbooks, non-teaching staff, and central office administrators, allowing more money to be spent on teachers (OECD, 2011; Tucker & Ruzzi, 2011).

Japan structures its school system to provide economically disadvantaged students more opportunities to excel. An OECD (2012a) report mentioned that Japan was one of 16 countries that assigned more teachers to disadvantaged schools to lower the student-teacher ratio in an effort to create more chances for these students to succeed. The same report mentioned that only Slovenia, Turkey, Israel, and the United States provided a higher student-teacher ratio for these students. Another practice that promotes equity is the rotation of teachers to different schools. Whereas in the United States students in low-socioeconomic districts are more likely to sit in classes with poorly qualified teachers than their more privileged counterparts, this outcome is much less likely to occur in Japan because every five to seven years teachers are assigned to a new school (Sclafani, 2017).

While in the United States students in low-socioeconomic areas usually attend schools with fewer educational resources, in Japan all students are funded equitably. Students who are ahead help those who struggle and do not skip grades, a practice that helps all students because those who tutor others often learn as much as those who are tutored. Further, the inequalities that result from tracking are nonexistent because this method of separating students is not implemented in Japan, resulting in classes that consist of students with varied skill levels (OECD, 2011; Tucker & Ruzzi, 2011).

Classes in Japanese schools consist of more students than those of many other countries. An OECD (2012b) report mentioned that although the average class size in OECD countries is 23 at the lower secondary level, Japan averages 32 students per class. School systems with small class sizes allow teachers more chances to personalize instruction to provide the guidance students need to excel academically. However, this approach is often a less efficient method than enhancing the quality of teaching. Further, many nations invested in improving the performance of their students by decreasing class sizes between 2000 and 2009, but only a few achieved this goal (OECD, 2012b).

Although the Japanese school year is longer than those of many other nations, with only six weeks of summer vacation, students do not go to school just for instruction. Indeed, they are given more breaks than students in many other countries. These breaks help keep students engaged to learn, providing them with the outdoor play and exercises they need to focus on academic work (OECD, 2011).

Cultural Values

Although the many components of Japanese education discussed so far contribute strongly to Japan's success in education, other countries hoping to achieve Japan's high scores in international testing cannot simply implement Japan's methods and expect to achieve similar results. Many of Japan's methods reflect cultural beliefs that have evolved over centuries.

Cultural values can vary greatly from country to country. American parents, for example, usually have different beliefs about the value of hard work than Japanese parents. Americans usually feel that inborn ability allows students to do outstanding work, but the Japanese tend to believe that outstanding results do not reflect innate abilities but plenty of effort (Stevenson & Stigler, 1992). Such beliefs explain why a large percentage of Japanese parents send their children to tutoring sessions, which usually last until the evening hours.

Another belief common in Japan that differs from traditional American values relates to the values they have for the group. Because America is a more individualistic country than Japan, Americans value the individual more than the group, but the Japanese put emphasis on the group over the individual. This value developed in part because the Japanese live in a threatening environment. Among the industrialized nations, Japan has few natural resources and one of the lowest proportions of arable land to population. The country experiences many natural disasters such as earthquakes and typhoons. These harsh conditions led the Japanese people to value cooperation more than people living in many Western nations. In order to survive, they believe that education and skills are as important as social relations and devotion to the group. As previously mentioned, the Japanese feel that if individuals devote all their efforts to the group, the group will respond in turn. However, society will have very little to offer individuals who reject the group (OECD, 2011; Tucker & Ruzzi, 2011).

The importance of working for the group rather than the individual manifests itself in the ways teachers are supported and evaluated. In addition, this belief influences the ways various individuals including family members, teachers, and even classmates take responsibility when a child fails to perform as expected. In such situations, the failure is viewed as a disappointment to the group. It harms the stature of the entire family, especially the mother. When an adolescent gets in trouble with the police, for example, the parents and the teacher are usually contacted and expected to respond (Baines & Yasuda, 2016).

The Japanese also respect the teaching profession. Teachers earn a salary comparable to Japan's highest paid civil servants and make as much as novice engineers when they start their careers (OECD, 2011).

Historical Origins of the Japanese Education System

While it is sometimes not feasible to expect that educational practices originating overseas will work in America, borrowing practices from abroad sometimes leads to progress. In fact, the Japanese reformed their system to a great extent by modeling the practices of nations with different value systems. A historical look at how the Japanese educational system evolved can be useful to further illustrate how such an approach can be practical. Japan not only borrowed educational methods that originated in European countries but also used John Dewey's ideas to reform its old system.

During the Tokugawa era (1603 to 1868), the Japanese lived in peace. The Samurai, who had the highest social status before this era, kept their status by becoming the officials who controlled the country. Japan prospered for many years during this era, but by its end, corruption and ineptitude plagued the government. The vulnerable regime collapsed in 1868 when a rebellion against the corruption occurred. After the overthrow, Japan borrowed ideas from the West to restructure its education system:

> Meiji Japan borrowed the administrative scheme for its new education system from the French (centralized and very orderly). From Germany they took the idea of an educational system built around a few elite national universities. England provided a model (in as public schools like Eaton and Harrow) of schools built around strong national moral principles. And the United States provided a powerful pedagogical model in the teachings of John Dewey, which the Japanese found congruent with their own idea of a school being responsible for developing the whole child as a family does. (Tucker & Ruzzi, 2011, p. 82)

The new leadership aimed to create universal education, believing the ine-qualities in the old system contributed to the decline of the old regime. The leadership intended to create chances for all Japanese people to benefit from education rather than to offer these opportunities only to the privileged. This philosophy contributed to the meritocratic society that constitutes modern day Japan.

In the 1880s, however, Japanese people began to fear that their nation would lose its traditional values by adopting ideas from elsewhere, resulting in a new focus on the Confucian virtues of respect for elders, loyalty, the need to educate oneself, and the obligation to obey the laws. Although the new focus emphasized the need to keep traditional Japanese values, Japan evaluated its education system by comparing it with those of other top-performing nations in education. After World War II, Japan continued its effort to create more opportunities for its people to earn a high-quality education by allowing all its high school graduates the chance to take the college entrance examinations. In previous years, the number of students allowed to take this test was restrict-ed (OECD, 2011; Tucker & Ruzzi, 2011).

Areas Needing Improvement

Although Japan implements many commendable educational practices, the country experiences its share of problems. While Harold Stevenson and James Stigler observed that elementary teachers engaged students and used methods that build problem-solving skills, other aspects of the educational system pro-mote rote methods of learning. The requirement of doing well on high school and college entrance examinations to enhance chances for future success is an example of such a practice. The views that some Americans have of Japa-nese youth as students who spend too much time memorizing information are therefore not entirely inaccurate.

Rote Learning Methods

High school entrance exams cause anxiety and stress to Japanese families, lead-ing people to refer to the process of preparing and taking these tests as "exam hell." Students experience anxiety because the high schools they attend can make a difference on which colleges will accept them. If students fail to perform well, they usually go to a school that lowers their chances of entering a top university. Therefore, poor test results can lower students' future employment opportunities. Further, these exams are believed to promote rote methods of study. The Central Council for Education recently criticized the use of these exams, arguing that they encourage memorization (Lewis, 2015).

When students reach the secondary level, the emphasis on rote methods of study persists as they hope to perform well on the grueling university entrance exams needed for admission to a top-ranked university. Doing poorly reduces opportunities for economic security and employment because attending a top university is essential for securing a good job in business or government (Yamaguchi, 2011).

Additionally, the approach to teaching many cram schools use to prepare students for these tests promotes rote learning. When students prepare for their high school entrance exams, for example, cram schools teach to the test by offering sample tests that match those students need to pass to attend their preferred school (Lewis, 2015).

Finally, the rigorous Japanese curriculum requires students to memorize a large number of facts, such as where rivers in remote areas are and when historical events outside of Japan occurred. Although the curriculum also requires students to solve problems and develops the skills they need to perform well on international tests like the PISA, students use rote-learning methods for the content they need to master (OECD, 2011; Tucker & Ruzzi, 2011).

Bullying

The pressure resulting from "exam hell" and the demanding curriculum is not the only form of stress many Japanese students endure. Countless students in Japan also withstand bullying, a problem that has increased considerably in the country in recent years. MEXT reported 224,540 cases of bullying in the 2015 academic year, a record high. Elementary schools experienced most of these cases with 151,190 incidents as junior high schools experienced 59,422 cases. High schools documented 12,654 incidents (McCrostie, 2017).

Many of these cases are severe, resulting in suicides. According to a study by Japan's Cabinet Office, more child suicides occur at the end of August and at the beginning of September, as well as during the middle of April. These are the times when schools reopen after students get a break. Officials therefore postulate that part of the problem originates in the schools and involves bullying. The bullying problem in Japan results to a great extent from the cultural values based on valuing the group over the individual. These values influence students to believe that conformity with the group is crucial. As a result, those who deviate from the norm usually suffer (Lu, 2015).

In Japan, the Asian aphorism "the nail that sticks out gets hammered down" is practiced to a certain extent through bullying tactics. The bullying in Japan is frequently more severe than in the United States because teachers sometimes participate. For example, one incident occurred when the class-mates of a fourth-grade boy began calling him "germ." When he told his teacher, the teacher started calling the boy names as well, leading this boy to stop going to school (McCrostie, 2017).

A survey spanning 10 months starting in April 2012 found that the num-ber of teachers who had used physical punishment on students had more than doubled from the whole fiscal year of 2011, rising from 404 cases to 840. At the time of the survey, this type of punishment was receiving more attention after a few cases were made public, with one involving a high school student who committed suicide after being beaten by his basketball coach (Torres, 2013).

The bullying problem in Japan is not new. An employee for an American newspaper took early retirement in 1986 and decided to explore Japan, work-ing there as an English teacher in a private school. He later wrote an article about the harsh and severe approach of discipline practiced in the country, describing how the adage "the nail that sticks out gets hammered down" is applied strictly in schools. He mentioned that although corporal punishment was illegal, teachers regularly practiced it and used fists, belts, and other con-venient weapons. This article described several shocking incidents including one that occurred on July 3, 1986, when a male homeroom teacher punished a 13-yearl-old-female student for being three minutes late by kicking her twice in the face and dislocating her jaw. A different incident occurred the same year on September 10th as 12 teachers kicked, slapped, and punched another 13-year-old-female for over three hours for riding a motorcycle for several hours on her summer break. This article also mentioned that as a result of teacher beatings, five students died from 1985 to 1990 (Young, 1993).

Creativity

The emphasis on conformity that contributes to the bullying problem is be-lieved to lead to a lack of creativity among Japanese students. For example, Japan had a lower score than the United States in the area of perceived entre-preneurial capabilities according to a 2011 Global Entrepreneurship Monitor

(GEM) report survey. Countries like Japan that do not tolerate deviating from the norm well and punish students for doing so tend to lack creativity and entrepreneurship capabilities. Focusing on entrepreneurship and innovation is crucial for progress. This focus encourages the type of thinking and action needed to find solutions for the world's most urgent problems, including creating jobs and using methods that promote sustainable development and advance the health of people (Zhao, 2012).

Nonetheless, the importance of creativity is debatable. Although Japan may be behind the United States in this arena, their educational system has created a strong workforce capable of constantly improving products on a vast scale. The Japanese value social order and view Western individualism as a cause of social disorder; therefore, they may not take the risks needed to produce as many innovations as Western nations. In assessing the importance of creativity as it relates to Japanese education, Marc Tucker and Betsy Brown Ruzzi (2011) asked whether it is better to have an occasional breakthrough or the continuous improvement of almost all aspects of society. Additionally, the creativity problem in Japan might be exaggerated because this country has been ranked very highly on the Global Innovation Index, which showed that Japan ranked right behind South Korea and the United states according to a 2008–2009 report (Tucker & Ruzzi, 2011).

Conclusion

Japan practices many methods that can enhance the American system. The most important of these involve equity for less fortunate students. Japan has a higher percentage of students from low-income families who perform well on the PISA than the United States. PISA refers to these students as "resilient" and describes them as pupils who come from a disadvantaged socioeconomic background but achieve much higher scores than would be predicted by their background. An OECD (2013) report showed that Japan had a much higher percentage of resilient students than the OECD average and that the United States had a lower percentage of these students than this average.

People in Japan usually do not make progress as a result of their connections like in many other countries. They become successful because they develop skills and talent through hard work. Although their system is fairer in this respect than those of many other nations, it is not perfect. There are inequalities that the poor endure. For example, many low-income parents cannot afford to spend as much on private instruction as those from higher income backgrounds. Thus, students from wealthier families usually get better positions because they have more opportunities to do better on the college entrance exams required to enter the best colleges and universities. Nonetheless, Japan provides low-income students with better teachers and educational resources than the United States does.

While this practice can and should be implemented in America, other methods used in Japan can improve the American system as well. However, some of these methods may not work as well in the United States. For example, the practices of strongly supporting new teachers and evaluating a team of teachers rather than individual teachers are more likely to work in Japan because Japanese mores are based on valuing the group over the individual. In the United States, on the other hand, more individualistic values prevail.

American policymakers also need to remember that Japan's strong emphasis on conformity will create similar problems in the United States as they do in Japan. The United States is often praised for its innovations while Japan is criticized for its lack of creativity. This outcome is due to the greater emphasis in the United States to tolerate new ways of accomplishing goals rather than to stress the use of traditional methods. In Japan, the low level to tolerate behavior that deviates from the norm leads to bullying. Some cases that tragically end in suicides involve teachers who bully students. While Japan's educational system includes commendable policies that Americans should implement, some of its other policies will worsen the United States' system. Borrowing the methods the Japanese implement that will enhance the American system is therefore the surefire way to proceed.

References

Ahn, R. (2014). How Japan supports novice teachers. *Educational Leadership*, 71(8), 49–53.

Ahn, R. (2016). Japan's communal approach to teacher induction: *Shokuin shitsu* as an indispensable nurturing ground for Japanese beginning teachers. *Teaching and Teacher Education*, 59, 420–430.

Ahn, R., Asanuma, S., & Mori, H. (2016). Japan's teachers earn tenure on day one. *Phi Delta Kappan*, 97(6), 27–31.

Allen, D. (2016). Japanese cram schools and entrance exam washback. *The Asian Journal of Applied Linguistics*, 3(1), 54–67.

Aoki, M. (2016, December 6). Japan's 15-year-olds perform well in PISA global academic survey. *The Japan Times*. Retrieved from http://www.japantimes.co.jp/news/2016/12/06/national/japans-15-year-olds-perform-well-pisa-global-academic-survey/#.WNK6M4U2s7A

Baines, L., & Yasuda, M. (2016). The high-achieving educational system of Japan. In H. Morgan & C. Barry (Eds.), *The world leaders in education: Lessons from the successes and drawbacks of their methods* (pp. 61–78). New York, NY: Peter Lang Publishing.

Clark, N. (2005). Education in Japan. *World Education News & Reviews*. Retrieved from http://wenr.wes.org/2005/05/wenr-mayjune-2005-education-in-japan

Darling-Hammond, L. (2010). *The flat world and education: How America's commitment to equity will determine our future*. New York, NY: Teachers College Press.

Fujita, H., & Dawson, W. P. (2007). The qualifications of the teaching force in Japan. In R. M. Ingersoll (Ed.), *A comparative study of teacher preparation and qualifications in six nations* (pp. 41–54). Philadelphia, PA: Consortium for Policy Research in Education.

Hatton, C. (2010). Respect for Japanese teachers means top results. *CBS News*. Retrieved from http://www.cbsnews.com/news/respect-for-japanese-teachers-means-top-results/

Lewis, C. (2015, February 15). Spare a thought for the junior-high students going through "exam hell." *The Japan Times*. Retrieved from http://www.japantimes.co.jp/community/2015/02/15/issues/spare-a-thought-for-the-junior-high-students-going-through-exam-hell/#.WOf5CYU2s7A

Lowe, R. J. (2015). Cram schools in Japan: The need for research. *The Language Teacher*, 39(1), 26–31.

Lu, S. (2015, October 22). The mystery behind Japan's high suicide rates among kids. *The Wilson Quarterly*. Retrieved from http://wilsonquarterly.com/stories/the-mystery-behind-japans-high-suicide-rates-among-kids/

McCrostie, J. (2017, January 25). Education in Japan in 2016: New solutions and age-old problems, from teaching English to bullying. *The Japan Times*. Retrieved from http://www.japantimes.co.jp/community/2017/01/25/issues/education-japan-2016-new-solutions-age-old-problems-teaching-english-bullying/#.WOfAk4U2s7C

Mirel, J., & Goldin, S. (2012). Alone in the classroom: Why teachers are too isolated. *The Atlantic*. Retrieved from https://www.theatlantic.com/national/archive/2012/04/alone-in-the-classroom-why-teachers-are-too-isolated/255976/

Mithout, A. (2016). Children with disabilities in the Japanese school system: A path toward social integration? *Contemporary Japan*, 28(2), 165–184.

Nagano, Y. (2014, August 10). A new ratio for the Japanese cram school. *The New York Times*. Retrieved from https://www.nytimes.com/2014/08/11/world/asia/a-new-ratio-for-the-japanese-cram-school.html?_r=0

Organization for Economic Co-operation and Development. (2011). *Strong performers and successful reformers in education: Lessons from PISA for the United States*. Paris: Organization of Economic Cooperation and Development.

Organization for Economic Co-operation and Development. (2012a). *Equity and quality in education: Supporting disadvantaged students and schools*. Paris: Organization of Economic Cooperation and Development.

Organization for Economic Co-operation and Development. (2012b). *Education Indicators in focus: How does class size vary around the world?* Retrieved from http://www.oecd.org/edu/skills-beyond-school/EDIF%202012--N9%20FINAL.pdf

Organization for Economic Co-operation and Development. (2013). *PISA 2012 results: Excellence through equity: Giving every student the chance to succeed (Volume II)*. Paris: Organization of Economic Cooperation and Development.

Otake, T. (2015). Public education spending in Japan lowest in OECD for sixth straight year. *The Japan Times*. Retrieved from http://www.japantimes.co.jp/news/2015/11/25/national/public-education-spending-japan-lowest-oecd-sixth-straight-year/#.WOmHtYU2s7B

Philips, O. (2015). Without janitors, students are in charge of keeping school shipshape. *NPR*. Retrieved from http://www.npr.org/sections/ed/2015/04/04/396621542/without-janitors-students-are-in-charge-of-keeping-school-shipshape

Sclafani, S. F. (2017). How the world recruits teachers. *Asia Society*. Retrieved from http://asiasociety.org/global-cities-education-network/how-world-recruits-teachers

Stevenson, H. W., & Stigler, J. (1992). *The Learning Gap: Why our schools are failing and what we can learn from Japanese and Chinese education*. New York, NY: Simon & Schuster.

Stewart, V. (2012). *A world-class education: Learning from international models of excellence and innovation*. Alexandria, VA: ASCD.

Torres, I. (2013, April 29). Survey shows 840 Japanese teachers used corporal punishment on students. *The Japan Daily Press*. Retrieved from http://japandailypress.com/survey-shows-840-japanese-teachers-used-corporal-punishment-on-students-2927909/

Tucker, M. S., & Ruzzi, B. B. (2011). Japan: Perennial league leader. In M. Tucker (Ed.), *Surpassing Shanghai: An agenda for American education built on the world's leading systems* (pp. 79–109). Cambridge, MA: Harvard Education Press.

Yamaguchi, M. (2011). Japan rattled by college entrance exam cheat case. *The Washington Post*. Retrieved from http://www.washingtonpost.com/wp-dyn/content/article/2011/03/04/AR2011030401324.html

Young, M (1993). The dark underside of Japanese education. *Phi Delta Kappan, 75*(2), 130–132.

Zhao, Y. (2012). Flunking innovation and creativity. *Phi Delta Kappan, 94*(1), 56–61.

· 5 ·

HIGH TEST SCORES COME
AT A HIGH PRICE

Education in South Korea

Policymakers can gain many insights by exploring the South Korean education system. Although this nation uses strategies that promote academic success, many of its students endure unfavorable consequences related to their academic environment. Korean students are sometimes described as having to deal with more pressure than any other students in the world. Although this country's educational system is often referred to as a pressure cooker for the stress placed on its students to perform highly in academics, it also implements commendable practices. These methods have helped students to consistently achieve some of the highest scores in the 21st century in international testing. On the 2015 PISA, for example, South Korea ranked 7th in reading, 7th in math, and 11th in science (Jackson & Kiersz, 2016).

A noteworthy aspect of South Korea's improvement in education involves the short time it took this nation to transform its school system from a poor system to one that ranks as highly as the top-performing systems in the world. An article published in 2008 about the best educational systems in the world mentioned that South Korea dramatically improved its educational system in a short time as the United States remained stagnant in this area:

According to the 2006 OECD data, the United States has fallen from 1st to 10th in the proportion of young adults with a high school degree or equivalent (including GED qualifications)—not because U.S. high school graduation rates dropped but because graduation rates rose so much faster elsewhere.... Looking at graduate output, the United States ranks only 18th among the 24 OECD countries with comparable data, with countries like Finland, Germany, Japan, and South Korea more than 15 percentage points ahead. (OECD, 2008)

South Korea illustrates the pace of progress that is possible (Uh, 2008). Two generations ago, the country had the economic output of Afghanistan today and ranked 24th in education output among the current 30 OECD countries. Today, South Korea is the world's top performer in secondary school graduation rates[.] (Schleicher & Stewart, 2008, p. 46)

In the 21st century, South Korea has enjoyed being known as the nation with the world's highest tertiary gross enrollment ratio. This ratio refers to the total enrollment in tertiary education, regardless of age as a percentage of the total population of the five-year age group continuing on from secondary school (Clark, 2013).

One of the reasons students in South Korea perform well on international tests has to do with the country's educational policies, which allow students to experience many favorable conditions that help them to excel. However, the strong emphasis on education reflected by parental attitudes that are often obsessive also explain why students excel academically. South Korean parents spend more on their children's education starting in the early years of schooling than most parents in other parts of the world. Consequently, children in South Korea spend more years in pre-primary school than their counterparts from around the world, helping them to excel academically in later years on international tests.

Early Childhood Education

Early childhood education is crucial because it reduces achievement gaps students may experience as they get older. In Korea, for example, the 2009 PISA analyses showed that students who went to pre-primary school for one year or more outperformed their counterparts without this experience by outscoring them on the PISA reading scale.

This trend occurs in other countries as well: Students in France, Belgium, Italy, and Israel receiving pre-primary education for over one year scored higher in reading than their counterparts without this education. In South Korea more students enroll in pre-primary school than in many other countries. According to the PISA 2009 analyses, 72% of students on average across OECD countries attended pre-primary school for over one year; however, 94% attended in Korea (OECD, 2014).

Families in South Korea spend more on pre-primary education than many parents in other nations. One reason they do so is that public expenditures for this level account for a very small percentage:

> On average across OECD countries, public expenditure on pre-primary education represents 0.47% of GDP, while private expenditure represents only 0.08% of GDP. Unlike all other OECD countries, in Korea, and, to a lesser extent, Japan, private expenditure represents a larger share of GDP devoted to pre-primary education than public expenditure.... In Korea, only 0.26% of GDP is spent on pre-primary education and public expenditures account for only 0.11% of the total, while 0.15% of the total is covered by private expenditures. (OECD, 2014, p. 79)

Attitudes toward Teachers and Education

Cultural attitudes toward teachers and education explain why parents pay more on pre-primary education than many parents living in other countries and why their children devote more time to academic work. These attitudes also explain the investment South Korea made in teachers that helped to transform its ineffective educational system to one that produced some of the world's most educated students. "Don't even step on the shadow of a teacher" is a Korean proverb that reflects the tremendous respect Korean people have for knowledge. Teachers along with priests were ranked as the most trusted members of the country according to one opinion poll. As a result of this respect, teachers are paid well, earning more than engineers. They earn salaries providing purchasing power in their economy that is much higher than those of American teachers (Darling-Hammond, 2010).

The high regard for education in South Korea leads parents to send their children to private academies or cram schools (called *hagwons*). Students in South Korea not only spend more hours of study but more days in school when compared with students in other regions of the world. For example, in contrast to the 180 days students spend in schools in the United States, students in South Korea spend 220. In addition, the average Korean child spends 13 hours a day studying according to some measures (Clark, 2013).

Consequently, many students experience the detrimental effects of spending too many hours of study. In an effort to reduce these long hours, South

Korean authorities put together a late-night patrol to alleviate the country's obsession with private tutoring by enforcing a curfew to stop children from studying past 10 p.m. A story in *Time* mentioned one case involving a cram school that violated the curfew, allowing about 10 teenagers to remain on the cram school's roof after 10 p.m. (Ripley, 2011).

Tutors who succeed in raising student test scores become stars, sometimes earning millions of dollars per year. One such tutor reported earning about 4 million dollars in one year for providing online language lessons, attributing part of his success to a motivating teaching style. One of the strategies he used to attract students included a pop song emphasizing that he could be trusted. Although his earnings seem impressive, they constitute only a fraction of the 20 billion dollars spent annually on private tutoring (Mundy, 2016).

Teacher Selection and Preparation

Although parental attitudes and the many hours students spend at cram schools contribute to students' high scores, teacher quality is also a factor. Teacher candidates in South Korea go through a rigorous teacher preparation and selection process.

Candidates hoping to become teachers normally enroll in a four-year undergraduate program; however, some graduate programs prepare candidates for teaching. To get hired, teachers need to complete a program that includes content and pedagogy. Then they need to take a two-part exam that measures their content and pedagogical knowledge. The exam includes performance elements and interviews as well as essay, short answer, and multiple-choice responses (Darling-Hammond, 2010).

Teacher shortage problems in South Korea do not exist because teachers are treated well. They receive not only good pay but also a lifetime certificate after completing the teacher preparation process, including automatic tenure after getting hired. Consequently, applicants face intense competition. Only 1 in 20 applicants for a teaching position, for example, secured a job in Seoul in 2008. At the secondary level, there are about five times as many candidates as available positions (Darling-Hammond, 2010).

Working Conditions

Teachers in South Korea are effective in part because they interact often with each other and receive sufficient hours of professional development. They have more opportunities to collaborate than American teachers because they spend less hours teaching. Whereas American teachers spend about 80% of their working time teaching, South Korean teachers only use about 35% for this purpose. When they are not teaching, teachers work together in an office to plan and to share instructional practices and ideas, a method especially beneficial for beginning teachers. This out-of-class time also helps teachers to solve problems and issues (Darling-Hammond, Wei, & Andree, 2010).

In addition, beginning teachers participate in a six-month induction program that provides them with support. They are also eligible to take in-service development courses for free. After their first four years, they need to take 90 hours of professional development courses every three years. They can also receive a salary increase after their third year if they obtain an advanced certificate by completing a five-week (180-hour) professional development program approved by the government (Darling-Hammond, 2010).

Equity in Education

South Korea has one of the world's highest percentages of students coming from socioeconomically disadvantaged backgrounds who perform well on the PISA. As mentioned in a previous chapter, PISA refers to such students as "resilient" and describes them as those who come from a low-income background but perform better than would be expected. According to an OECD (2013) report, over half of all socioeconomically disadvantaged students in Korea fall in this category.

One reason that low-income students perform better academically in Korea than in many other nations has to do with the equitable distribution of educational resources. Whereas low-income students in the United States usually face severe educational inequalities in school, in Korea more educational opportunities exist for these students:

> Korea guarantees that students in all schools enjoy similar resources. Advantaged and disadvantaged schools in Korea have similar proportions of full-time teachers, face similar problems with respect to teacher shortages, and have the same percentage of qualified teachers and of teachers with university-level degrees among all full-time teachers. In around half of OECD countries, disadvantaged schools tend to have

more teachers per student. Korea is one of these countries....The ratio of computers to students is also higher in disadvantaged schools in Korea than in many other countries, suggesting that Korea is attempting to develop an infrastructure that will ensure that socio-economic disadvantage does not translate in fewer opportunities to learn and that schools actively try to reduce the effect of social inequalities on academic achievement. These findings suggest that Korea ensures an equitable distribution of human resources, both in the quantity of resources and in their quality. (OECD, 2014, p. 47)

One of the ways South Korea creates equal educational opportunities for low-income students is by providing incentives for professionals to serve in areas difficult to staff. Educators serving in such areas receive bonus points toward promotion. Other incentives include stipends, less in-class teaching time, and smaller class sizes (Darling-Hammond, 2010).

School Structure

The Korean education system is based on six years of primary school, three years of middle school, three years of high school, and four years of undergraduate education. School is compulsory for children between the ages of 6 and 15. Students have little choice regarding which school they can go to until they complete middle school. They usually attend their local elementary and junior high schools (Clark, 2013).

Primary and Middle School Education

Korea offers education for free for children in grades one through six. English is assigned for one hour per week to third and fourth graders and for two hours to fifth and sixth graders. Primary students take ethics, Korean language, science, social studies, mathematics, physical education, music, and the arts as core subjects (Clark, 2013).

As with primary school, middle school is compulsory and free. Students are grouped according to ability in mathematics, social studies, science, English, and Korean language. However, they are not streamed according to ability for moral education, physical education, fine arts, practical arts, and music. They can also take optional courses, including home economics, foreign languages, technology, and environmental education (Clark, 2013).

High School

Different types of high schools are available for students in South Korea, including academic and vocational schools. While primary and middle school education is free and compulsory, the three-year high school period is not. However, over 99% of students continue from middle school to high school, with the majority attending academic high schools (Clark, 2013).

The process of admission varies across school systems. In some areas, referred to as "equalization areas," students are assigned to schools through a computer lottery system. In other areas, students are admitted according to academic achievement and entrance examinations. During their first year, students are required to take 10 subjects, including Korean language, social studies, ethics, mathematics, and science. During their second year, they choose their major areas of study or vocational training. Students in vocational high schools take general secondary education their first year followed by specialized courses in agriculture, industry, commerce, fisheries, and home economics their second year (Clark, 2013).

For high school graduates to enter a university, they need to take the College Scholastic Ability Test (CSAT) offered each year by the Korea Institute for Curriculum and Evaluation. The exam is available in one of three streams: social studies, sciences, or vocational education. Although an effort was made in 2008 to reduce the importance of this exam, the results of the CSAT still play a huge role in determining students' future education prospects. Consequently, students often endure tremendous pressure when preparing for this exam (Clark, 2013).

The Teaching and Learning Environment

Although South Korea implements some commendable practices, the pressure for students to do well on the CSAT leads to devastating consequences. While some scholars praise the methods Korea implements to achieve its status as a world-class nation in education, other researchers are critical of the South Korean educational system for good reasons. These reasons include the rote methods of study the college entrance exam promotes and the tremendous stress placed on students to perform well on this exam (Park, 2012).

Many South Korean students withstand unusually high stress levels when attempting to gain admission to one of the nation's top three universities—

Seoul National University, Korea University, and Yonsei University. The reason for this pressure involves the privileges students gain by graduating from one of these universities. These privileges include getting the best jobs, the right spouse, and important connections (Park, 2015).

Because the competition to be admitted to one of these universities is fierce and because a high score on the college entrance exam is crucial, K–12 teachers tend to implement inferior methods of teaching. They often concentrate on rote methods of teaching as they neglect creativity, discussion, and self-expression. Because physical education is not as important in Korean schools as it is in American schools, there is a shortage of high-quality gymnasiums. Most teachers teach primarily to prepare students for content that will appear on the entrance examination. This exam is important not only because of the strong emphasis universities place on it for admitting students but also because of the limited opportunities students have to take it. Unlike the American SAT, students can take it only once a year. Consequently, preparation sometimes starts as early as kindergarten (Park, 2012).

An approach to education that devotes little time to creativity, discussion, and self-expression and promotes excessive hours of study harms students in several ways. Park (2015) reported that South Korea's middle school students sleep an average of 6 hours and 35 minutes a night and that high school students sleep an average of 5 hours and 45 minutes. The stress involving academic competition contributes to high suicide rates. For example, 2012 South Korean government data showed that young people between the ages of 9 and 24 died as a result of suicide more often than any other cause of death (Park, 2015).

Other conditions associated with excessive hours of studying include myopia, curvature of the spine, and forward head posture syndrome. A recent study found that about one in seven children in a wealthy Seoul district suffers from curvature of the spine. Additionally, at least three out of four high school pupils in Seoul are myopic, and physicians are reporting high numbers of students with forward head posture syndrome (Mundy, 2016).

Although Barack Obama praised the Korean approach to education more than once, many Koreans are dissatisfied with their school system for its lack of creativity and heavy reliance on private tutoring. One reason South Korea has one of the world's lowest birthrates involves the unhappiness many parents feel toward the psychological and financial costs of the country's educational approach (Onishi, 2008).

The strong dependence on tutoring creates problems even when Korean students enter top American universities. Although Koreans do well on international tests, they often fail to graduate from top American universities. The dropout rates of Korean students illustrate this point and show that 44% of Korean students who go to top American universities fail to graduate. This dropout rate is much higher than the rate of Chinese students (25%) and of students from India (21%). The excessive hours Korean students spend studying may help them score highly on university entrance exams, but the rote methods they frequently use do little to help them develop the skills needed to succeed in American universities. Dr. Samuel Kim of Columbia University attributes part of this problem to the lack of participation in extracurricular activities. Whereas Korean students spend about 25% of their time participating in extracurricular activities, students from other countries use about twice as much time for these activities. Extracurricular activities are believed to play an important role in acclimating foreign students to American society (Park, 2012).

The "Wild Geese" Phenomenon

The dissatisfaction many Korean parents feel toward their education system has led many of them to send their children abroad for education. This phenomenon, sometimes referred to as "wild geese families," occurs when mothers move to English-speaking countries like the United States to school their children as the fathers stay in South Korea. An article in the *New York Times* reported that according to the Korean Educational Development Institute, 29,511 children left South Korea in 2006, about twice as many as in 2004 and almost seven times the number in 2000. One reason for this consequence is that many parents believe' Korean schools are failing to teach creative thinking skills (Onishi, 2008).

In addition to the methods schools apply to prepare students for the national exam, Koreans are dissatisfied with what their children learn at cram schools. A professor of English at Seoul National University mentioned that while students may learn how to pass exams at cram schools, they do not learn how to analyze and think critically. Failing to gain these skills lowers their chances for future success (Goh-Grapes, 2009).

Although many families send their children abroad for education, the ultimate goal is for the children to return with a superior education that will allow them to enter one of Korea's top universities. Unfortunately, "wild geese families" endure tremendous stress as a result of being separated from each other. Many children with weak English skills have difficulty fitting in while their mothers become depressed from being separated from their husbands. Fathers also suffer. An online survey found that over 70% of "wild goose" fathers mentioned experiencing high levels of depression, alcohol problems, and poor nutrition (Reed, 2015).

Historical Background

Although the education system in South Korea causes problems, educational leaders can still learn from the methods this nation implemented that created tremendous progress in education. A historical look at how Korea accomplished its success in education is useful for this reason.

Japanese Occupation (1910–1945)

Japan colonized Korea in 1910 and controlled key positions in the civil service and in the educational system. The colonial bureaucracy employed over twice as many Japanese workers as Koreans in 1942, relegating Koreans to low-level clerical positions. Japanese colonial education was intended to assimilate Koreans in a way to keep them subordinate to the Japanese. All students including Koreans were taught in Japanese, with Koreans strongly restricted from enrolling in secondary education (Sorensen, 1994).

Cultural nationalists believed that widespread modern education would help Koreans to regain their independence. Although in 1942 about 40% of Korean children attended elementary school, fewer than 5% continued to middle school. The few students continuing to middle schools did not attend the same schools as those the Japanese students attended. Even after Koreans demanded tertiary education, they were underrepresented. For example, Keijō Imperial University opened in Seoul in 1924 in response to Korean demands but enrolled more Japanese than Korean students (Sorensen, 1994).

South Korea as an Independent Nation

South Korea was a nation of illiterate or semi-literate peasants in 1945. Although it had gained independence from Japan, only 40% of students in grades one through six were enrolled in school. A very small percentage of the population (5%) had a secondary school education. Only one university existed in the country. The lack of opportunities for families to educate their children during Japanese occupation frustrated families and contributed to the zeal for education that has persisted until today. Even poor parents were willing to make tremendous sacrifices to send their children to school. The pent-up demand for education led to the opening of hundreds of new schools at all levels (Seth, 2016).

However, the new schools had problems accommodating the increasing number of students. The state could not offer adequate financial aid shortly after its independence because it still had not enjoyed the rapid economic growth that would come years later. Consequently, classes were large, often including more than 100 students. Schools in crowded urban areas operated under two or three shifts a day. Quality therefore was compromised (Sorensen, 1994).

Additionally, the country endured many problems shortly after its independence, including a civil war that lasted from 1950 to 1953 and political turmoil that ended with a military coup in 1961. Despite these problems, educational development occurred quickly. Enrollment increased considerably from 1945 to 1960 in primary schools, secondary schools, and higher education. Ninety-six percent of children of primary school age were attending school by 1960. By the 1970s, almost all students were attending middle school (Seth, 2016).

The Development of the School System

In developing its school system, Korea first concentrated on educating younger children by allocating educational resources to primary education. When universal primary education was achieved, the government increased its attention to secondary education, leading to its expansion in the 1960s and 1970s. Priority was first offered to middle schools, then to high schools (Seth, 2016).

Some of the ways Korea attempted to fulfill its goal of creating equal access to education included implementing a policy in the 1950s designed to assign teachers to different schools every five years and to invest in rural schools. The state also created a uniform curriculum. These strategies worked. Although students in schools in major cities averaged higher test scores, the differences in test scores and other aspects of schooling among urban and rural areas and within school districts were usually lower than in many other nations (Seth, 2016).

Korea also attempted to reduce inequalities by implementing the High School Equalization Policy (HSEP) in 1973. This policy assigns students to high schools in their residential areas according to a random computerized lottery. One reason the policy was proposed was to reduce excessive competition to enter elite high schools. In the late 1960s and early 1970s, secondary students were allowed to choose schools due to a free competition system. This system led to severe inequalities as a few elite high schools emerged and selected only top-tier students. Such a system promoted inequalities involving academic ability, socioeconomic background, and teacher quality (Byun, Kim, & Park, 2012).

Resistance toward the HSEP emerged despite its perceived effectiveness in reducing differences between schools and lowering the large amounts of money parents were paying for their children to enter elite schools. Several concerns led to its resistance. First, the HSEP restricted students' and parents' chances to select schools. Second, teachers experienced more difficulty when teaching because their pupils varied greatly in academic ability. Although the HSEP continued to expand after these controversies emerged, in the 1990s some cities abolished it. Since 2000, an increasing number of education district offices have adopted the HSEP. About 25 major cities implemented the HSEP in 2009, accounting for over half of the academic high school student population in Korea (Byun et al., 2012).

Another important feature involving the way Korea structured its school system involved teacher training. While the country lacked qualified teachers in the late 1940s and from the 1950s into the 1960s, it did not quickly train them. Instead, it made teacher education programs highly selective and competitive. Teachers were also trained intensively. Consequently, South Korea had a large number of highly trained educators for a country at its income level but still needed more as a result of the tremendous demand for education. The result was large classroom sizes (Seth, 2016). Even today South Korea has one of the highest average class sizes in the world. An OECD (2012) report indicated that Korea averages over 32 students per class at the lower secondary school level, well above the OECD average of 23 students per class.

Areas in Need of Improvement

South Korea is one of the top-performing countries in education in need of more improvement than many other high-achieving nations. The reason relates to the many problems this country experiences that result directly from the obsession families have to educate their children. These problems put students under tremendous pressure, promote high levels of rote learning, and lead to widespread cheating.

High Stress Levels

The high stress levels placed on students to succeed academically contribute to a plethora of problems for Korean children. Many of these problems stem from the school environment. One such problem is bullying. One suicide in 2013 shocked the country as a 15-year-old high school student jumped to his death from an apartment in the city of Gyeongsan after being bullied for about two years. The boy had written a suicide note naming five students he believed had bullied him and mentioning that bullies would never be caught because violence occurs in unsupervised areas. As mentioned previously, suicide in South Korea is the leading cause of death among Korean youth. It is believed that one of the reasons for this high rate is directly linked to bullying and family problems (Yoo, 2013).

The high level of pressure students endure leads to student unhappiness as well. Researchers at Yonsei University published a report showing that South Korean youth are the unhappiest students when compared with those in other OECD nations. Students ranging from elementary school children to those in the high school grades participated in a survey. They scored at the very bottom of the happiness scale for six consecutive years since the survey was first conducted in 2009. South Korea had managed to avoid the bottom spot in 2015 but dropped to last place again in 2016 (Eun-joo, 2016).

A 2014 opinion article in the *New York Times* was highly critical of the pressure packed education system in South Korea. The article mentioned that although the system produces high scores, it does so as students pay a stiff price that compromises important aspects of childhood development:

> The world may look to South Korea as a model for education—its students rank among the best on international education tests—but the system's dark side casts a long shadow. Dominated by Tiger Moms, cram schools and highly authoritarian teachers, South Korean education produces ranks of overachieving students who pay a stiff price in health and happiness. The entire program amounts to child abuse. It should be reformed and restructured without delay. (Koo, 2014, para. 5)

This article was about a family who moved from Korea to Vancouver to avoid the continued pressure that had caused a family member to become ill. It mentioned that most families put unrelenting pressure on children and that competition since the 1990s had increased. The author, who returned to Korea 13 years after leaving, described that children's eyes appeared dead as they were being taught advanced English grammar at a cram school. When asked if they were happy, one of them expressed a desire for her mother to leave because the child felt that she did nothing but nag her about academic performance (Koo, 2014).

Cheating

The intense and competitive environment leads to cheating problems in some Asian countries, especially in South Korea and China. For example, the SAT exam was cancelled in all of South Korea in 2013 due to cheating. Cheating also occurred with the ACT exam, resulting in the cancellation of this exam for all test takers in the country in 2016. Both cases involved the leaking of test questions (Stecklow, 2016).

Even parents may participate. The cheating process starts at testing centers as staff members leak the material to cram schools shortly before exams. The cram schools then select parents and students to contact. Middlemen also participate and go back and forth from schools to parents as they buy and sell test papers. A lecturer at a South Korean school recalled a time when a parent offered him $25,000 to send exam questions to her son. The plan involved taking the test in the United States and using the difference in time zones to send test answers in advance (Harris, 2016).

Students in South Korea cheat not only when taking exams to enter American universities but also when taking the national exam to enter Korean universities. In 2005, for example, the country faced a large cheating scandal when officials discovered that 20 cheating rings had text-messaged answers to students to help them pass the national college entrance exam (Vencat, 2006).

Rote Learning

The pressure to succeed academically that contributes to cheating also promotes excessive hours of study at cram schools. Although some cram school teachers experiment with innovative methods of teaching, many schools rely on rote methods, reducing the chances to prepare students for the many challenges they will deal with in the real world. Even a former minister of education said that cram schools rely on rote learning and that this style of teaching could lead to problems in developing other skills like creativity and critical thinking (Fifield, 2014).

The do-or-die exam system in South Korea also contributes to rote learning, especially during the high school years. Many students at this level experience what is often described as "examination hell," a harsh approach involving cramming and rote memorization of facts. Students use such an approach because the consequences of poor performance include a lack of opportunities for future success (Park, 2012).

Conclusion

South Korea, like other top-performing nations in education, implements many commendable practices that allow this country to rank consistently among the leading countries in education. In addition, the country's average annual public expenditure per student on education is relatively low, below the amount the United States spends (National Center for Education Statistics, 2016). Some of the methods this nation used to transform itself into a country with some of the world's highest-scoring test takers include selecting teachers carefully, training them well, and providing equity in education.

Unfortunately, one of the crucial components of this nation's success in education is difficult, and maybe even impossible, to implement in the United States. This component is Korea's zeal toward education. Often described as an obsession, Korean people's attitudes toward education can be understood from a historical perspective because the severe inequalities this nation withstood before its independence led to a tremendous passion for education that has persisted to the present.

Other aspects of the Korean education system involve the problems associated with the obsessive desire its people have to perform well academically. These problems harm its young people to a great extent and cause many Korean parents to leave their country. No country should want to inherit such problems.

The only way for South Koreans to get the best positions in their nation is by graduating from one of the best universities. Families are therefore under high levels of pressure. They pay a great deal of money to send their children to cram schools and expect hard work from their children, resulting in extremely long hours of study. In 2012, for example, parents spent about

$17 billion for tutoring, considerably more than the $5 to $7 billion spent on private tutors in the United States in 2010 (Nuwer, 2013).

South Korean youth pay a heavy toll for the pressure they endure. It is believed the reason this nation has the highest suicide rate in the world and the second highest youth suicide rate among OECD members is directly linked to the Korean academic system. This system is criticized not only for the stress it places on students but also for the memorization it promotes. A teacher who had worked in the country for a decade mentioned that educators know the emphasis on tests fails to prepare students for the global market (Sistek, 2013).

Therefore, policymakers cannot simply look at a nation's test scores and decide to implement its policies in another country with lower scores. Korea's education system may be the best example to emphasize this point. In addition, Korean families' obsession with education reflects the country's unique history. Their attitude toward education cannot be applied overseas easily. Although their zeal contributes to high scores, it also leads to many problems. Many of the practices used in Korea would worsen the education systems of other countries rather than enhance them because the Korean system lacks some crucial components of outstanding educational systems. One of these components involves the implementation of a style of teaching that emphasizes critical thinking and minimizes rote learning.

References

Byun, S., Kim, K., & Park, H. (2012). School choice and educational inequality in South Korea. *Journal of School Choice*, 6(2), 158–183.

Clark, N. (2013). Education in South Korea. *World Education News & Reviews*. Retrieved from http://wenr.wes.org/2013/06/wenr-june-2013-an-overview-of-education-in-south-korea

Darling-Hammond, L. (2010). *The flat world and education: How America's commitment to equity will determine our future*. New York, NY: Teachers College Press.

Darling-Hammond, L., Wei, R. C., & Andree, A. (2010). How high-achieving countries develop great teachers. *Stanford Center for Opportunity Policy in Education*. Retrieved from https://edpolicy.stanford.edu/sites/default/files/publications/how-high-achieving-countries-develop-great-teachers.pdf

Eun-joo, J. (2016, May 3). South Korean youngsters back at the bottom of OECD happiness rank. *The Hankyoreh*. Retrieved from http://english.hani.co.kr/arti/english_edition/e_business/742307.html

Fifield, A. (2014, December 30). In education-crazy South Korea, top teachers become multimillionaires. *The Washington Post*. Retrieved from https://www.washingtonpost.com/world/

asia_pacific/in-education-crazy-south-korea-top-teachers-become-multimillionaires/201 4/12/29/1bf7e7ae-849b-11e4-abcf-5a3d7b3b20b8_story.html?utm_term=.0c96749cf737

Goh-Grapes, A. (2009, February 22). Phenomenon of wild goose fathers in South Korea. *The Korea Times*. Retrieved from http://www.koreatimes.co.kr/www/news/nation/2009/02/117_40060.html

Harris, B. (2016, December 3). Rampant cheating closes US university exam centres in South Korea. *Financial Times*. Retrieved from https://www.ft.com/content/b6084bf6-a733-11e6-8b69-02899e8bd9d1

Jackson, A., & Kiersz, A. (2016). The latest ranking of top countries in math, reading, and science is out—and the US didn't crack the top 10. *Business Insider*. Retrieved from http://www.businessinsider.com/pisa-worldwide-ranking-of-math-science-reading-skills-2016-12

Koo, S. (2014, August 1). An assault upon our children: South Korea's education system hurts students. *The New York Times*. Retrieved from https://www.nytimes.com/2014/08/02/opinion/sunday/south-koreas-education-system-hurts-students.html

Mundy, S. (2016, June 16). South Korea's millionaire tutors. *Financial Times*. Retrieved from https://www.ft.com/content/c0b611fc-dab5-11e3-9a27-00144feabdc0

National Center for Education Statistics. (2016). *Education expenditures by country*. Retrieved from https://nces.ed.gov/programs/coe/indicator_cmd.asp

Nuwer, R. (2013, August 8). Tutors in South Korea, paid according to popular demand, can earn millions. *Smithsonian Magazine*. Retrieved from http://www.smithsonianmag.com/smart-news/tutors-in-south-korea-paid-according-to-popular-demand-can-earn-millions-26433555/

Onishi, N. (2008, June 8). For English studies, Koreans say goodbye to dad. *The New York Times*. Retrieved from http://www.nytimes.com/2008/06/08/world/asia/08geese.html

Organization for Economic Co-operation and Development. (2012). *Education indicators in focus: How does class size vary around the world?* Retrieved from http://www.oecd.org/edu/skills-beyond-school/EDIF%202012--N9%20FINAL.pdf

Organization for Economic Co-operation and Development. (2013). *PISA 2012 results: Excellence through equity: Giving every student the chance to succeed* (Vol. II). Paris: Organization of Economic Cooperation and Development.

Organization for Economic Co-operation and Development. (2014). *Strong performers and successful reformers in education: Lessons from PISA for Korea*. Paris: Organization of Economic Cooperation and Development.

Park, R. (2015, July 1). South Korea's young social entrepreneurs: A solution to a broken education system? *Kennedy School Review*. Retrieved from http://harvardkennedyschoolreview.com/south-korea-social-entrepreneurs/

Park, S. H. (2012). Why the Korean school system is not superior. *New Politics*. Retrieved from http://newpol.org/content/why-korean-school-system-not-superior

Reed, B. (2015, June 16). "Wild geese families": Stress, loneliness for South Korean families heading overseas to gain edge in "brutal" education system. *Australian Broadcasting Commission*. Retrieved from http://www.abc.net.au/news/2015-06-16/thousands-of-south-korea-families-apart-for-australian-education/6547604

Ripley, A. (2011, September 25). Teacher, leave those kids alone. *Time*. Retrieved from http://content.time.com/time/magazine/article/0,9171,2094427,00.html

Schleicher, A., & Stewart, V. (2008). Learning from world-class schools. *Educational Leadership*, 66(2), 44–51.

Seth, M. J. (2016). South Korea's education: A national obsession. In H. Morgan & C. Barry (Eds.), *The world leaders in education: Lessons from the successes and drawbacks of their methods* (pp. 107–125). New York, NY: Peter Lang Publishing.

Sistek, H. (2013, December 8). South Korean students wracked with stress. *Al Jazeera*. Retrieved from http://www.aljazeera.com/indepth/features/2013/12/south-korean-students-wracked-with-stress-201312884628494144.html

Sorensen, C. W. (1994). Success and education in South Korea. *Comparative Education Review*, 38(1), 10–35.

Stecklow, S. (2016, June 10). ACT cancels entrance exam in South Korea, Hong Kong after test leak. *Reuters*. Retrieved from http://www.reuters.com/article/us-usa-college-cheating-idUSKCN0YX008

Vencat, E. F. (2006, March 26). The perfect score. *Newsweek*. Retrieved from http://www.newsweek.com/perfect-score-106425

Yoo, A. (2013, March 17). South Korea rattled by suicide of bullied teen. *Time*. Retrieved from http://world.time.com/2013/03/17/south-korea-rattled-by-suicide-of-bullied-teen/

· 6 ·

CHINA'S SUCCESS IN EDUCATION

Is This Nation Really That Good?

China's recent rankings in international testing are impressive but also misleading. The controversy involves comparing parts of China with entire nations. Unlike most other countries of the world, China releases its PISA results only from certain parts of the country. This practice leads journalists to misinterpret the scores and to suggest that all of China is surpassing other countries rather than only certain parts of the nation. In 2009, for example, *Time* published a story with a headline stating that China had beaten Finland for the top marks in education instead of announcing that only Shanghai had accomplished this goal (Loveless, 2013a).

For the 2015 PISA, mainland China released the scores of three more provinces (Beijing, Jiangsu, and Guangdong). The previous doubt about using Shanghai's scores as an indication for how all of China is performing on the PISA may therefore subside because the four provinces releasing their results have a combined population of 226 million people. Although the combined average results of these four provinces failed to put China at the very top, they were high enough to rank these areas among the leading countries in math and science:

> The average score for all four provinces places China near the very top of the global rankings in mathematics and science. Their combined scores would have placed Chi-

na in the top ten were it not for their scores in reading, which were about the same as the average U.S. score for reading. (Tucker, 2016, para. 2)

Despite this accomplishment, the regions that released their 2015 PISA results represent only a small portion of China's population because the country's total population consists of over 1 billion people. Because these four provinces represent less than a quarter of the Chinese population, questions should still arise as to whether these regions accurately represent the entire country. Although releasing scores from only certain regions is still problematic, the four provinces that performed well deserve attention because they contain almost two-thirds of the population of the United States but outperformed it on the PISA.

This chapter explores the educational system of China as well as the differences in educational opportunities between Shanghai, a region where students have performed very well on the PISA, and the poor rural parts of China, where scores are not revealed. But first, the chapter focuses on more of the problems that relate to comparing parts of China with entire nations. An example that sheds light on these concerns involves what critics said after the 2009 PISA results were released.

Unfair Comparisons

Shanghai's education system deserves attention because this region ranked first in the world on the PISA both in 2009 and 2012 in all three subjects this assessment measures: reading, math, and science. When Shanghai's scores were released in 2009, many Americans, including President Obama, expressed concern that American schools were underperforming. However, critics raised valid concerns about comparing Shanghai with entire nations because it contains a very small percentage (less than 3%) of China's total population. In addition, this region attracts students more likely to go to college than students in other parts of China. About 24% of all Chinese students attend college, but almost 84% of students in Shanghai achieve this goal (Loveless, 2013a).

Further, families from Shanghai tend to be much wealthier than those in other parts of China, spending much more money on their children's education outside of school than less privileged families in rural areas. Although students in the provinces outside of Shanghai took the PISA in 2009, the Chinese government permitted only the release of scores from Shanghai. Additionally, schools in poor rural areas in China, where a considerable number of students live, offer fewer opportunities for a good education than schools in Shanghai (Loveless, 2013a).

The Chinese Educational System

Despite the problems of comparing only the parts of China that perform well to entire countries, policymakers can gain valuable information from these regions because few other areas of the world perform as well on international tests. Since the 2009 PISA test, China has also implemented new policies in an effort to improve its system. To gain insights about Chinese policies that may improve the American system and the ones that may harm it, it is important to have an awareness of various components of the Chinese system.

China's education system is the largest in the world, with about 260 million students. The country employs over 15 million teachers in about 514,000 schools (OECD, 2016a). Like many top-performing nations, China has a nine-year compulsory education system, requiring students at the primary and lower secondary levels to attend school. To become teachers, candidates need to take the Teachers' Qualification Examination, which evaluates important aspects of teaching, including pedagogic skills, content knowledge, and professional ethics. Teachers need to take more than 360 hours of training every five years to renew their certificates (OECD, 2016b). Although the Ministry of Education creates the major education policies, provincial education departments have control at the local level and implement the policies under the guidelines of the state regulations (Michael, 2016).

Early Childhood Education

Chinese students typically enroll in preschool starting at age 2 and remain enrolled until age 6. Although preschool is not compulsory, the government is aiming to increase its availability so that by 2020 all students have access to schools at this level. To accomplish this goal, governments at the local level have implemented the Three-Year Preschool Education Action Plan, a law that requires more funding to be available for preschools. In addition, the central government has urged private groups and people to form private kindergartens. Such efforts have led to an increase in enrollment. In 2014, for example, the three-year preschool education gross enrollment rate reached 70%, increasing almost 20% over five years (OECD, 2016a).

The Ministry of Education has also created documents to improve the quality of preschool education. These documents focus on managing kindergartens and include regulations and professional standards for teachers to improve oversight of key aspects of kindergarten education (OECD, 2016a).

Primary and Lower Secondary Education

The curriculum at the elementary level emphasizes general education and includes moral education, mathematics, Chinese language, arts, and physical education. During the third grade, students start to take science and English and also cover topics such as innovative research, information technology, community service, and labor education. After graduating, they attend junior high school without having to take exams (Michael, 2016).

Before the 21st century, lower secondary schools admitted students based on the results of an entrance exam. However, to implement compulsory education at the junior high school level and to provide a more holistic approach of education, a policy of mandatory enrollment superseded the exam (OECD, 2016a). At the lower secondary level, more subjects are added to the general education courses. These subjects include foreign language, biology, physics, chemistry, history, geography, and music (Michael, 2016).

Upper Secondary Education

After compulsory education, students may choose to continue to the senior secondary level. Five types of senior secondary schools exist: general senior secondary, technical or specialized secondary, adult secondary, vocational secondary, and crafts schools. General senior secondary schools are regular high schools, but the other types focus on vocational education. In order to attend, students need to take an exam called the *Zhongkao*. Their exam scores are important because admission to high school depends on how well they score. In addition, they are assigned to different schools based on their scores.

In the recent past, China has made rapid progress in increasing participation at secondary schools. In 2014, for example, an overwhelming percentage of students (95%) continued from lower secondary school to the senior secondary level, but a much lower percentage (40%) continued to this level in 2005. This progress occurred in part as a result of efforts to increase enrollment at vocational schools, which enrolled just under 22% of the number of students attending senior secondary schools in 2014 (OECD, 2016a).

Regular High Schools

Regular high schools usually require students to pick between a science stream and an art stream of study before they begin the 11th grade. To graduate, they need to earn credits based on completing modules. For each module they complete, students earn two credits. To advance to a higher grade, a minimum number of credits must be completed.

Students need to complete a minimum of 144 credits to receive a high school diploma. In addition, students need to pass one of two exams: the General Examination for High School Students (*huikao*) or the Academic Proficiency Test (APT). The provincial authorities administer these exams and include all subjects in the curriculum. To enroll in a regular university, students need to take a test called the *gaokao*, a difficult college entrance examination (Michael, 2016).

Vocational High Schools

The vocational curriculum includes both academic and vocational subjects. Mandatory subjects include mathematics, Chinese, computer applications, and physical education. Specialty courses, teaching practice, and a comprehensive internship constitute the vocational courses. Hours of study are evenly distributed between theory learning and practice (Michael, 2016).

Education in Shanghai

Schools in the Chinese educational system can vary greatly from each other. For this reason, I will next compare two parts of the country with schools that differ considerably—Shanghai and the rural areas—to highlight the differences in educational opportunities these regions offer. Shanghai is recognized as an area that has some of the world's highest scoring students in international testing. The reason has to do with how well they ranked according to the six levels PISA uses to evaluate student performance. On the 2009

PISA, for example, 27% of students in Shanghai scored at the highest level in mathematics, a higher percentage than any other region of the world. This percentage was well above any other top-performing system (Tucker, 2011).

How does Shanghai achieve such good results? One reason involves its rigorous approach to teaching. For example, Shanghai applies "teaching-study groups" daily to improve instruction. These groups involve meetings with relevant personnel who create thorough lesson plans on a given topic for the following week. Teachers then provide instruction based on these plans but also modify them into more detailed lesson plans for other teachers. These plans guide teachers when teaching and also serve as documentation of their professional performance.

Other forms of collaboration occur when teachers observe each other. For example, new teachers learn when experienced teachers observe them and provide feedback. Sometimes teachers teach demonstration lessons to a large number of teachers. This strategy allows the sharing of knowledge on aspects of teaching and learning, thereby improving instruction (OECD, 2014).

Teacher Qualifications and Professional Development in Shanghai

Shanghai has recently increased the qualifications needed to teach. Currently, all teachers at the secondary level hold a degree and professional certification, while those at the primary level are required to have a sub-degree diploma.

Shanghai also has a rigorous system of professional development. Teachers need to take 240 hours of professional development within five years and to show improvement in their professional capacities. This approach differs from merely monitoring their professional activities because they are provided with more responsibility and viewed as capable of handling any difficult student situation (OECD, 2014).

In addition, teachers can be promoted to higher ranks by helping other teachers succeed. As part of the national system, teachers in Shanghai get ranked according to four levels and get promoted according to their ability to provide demonstration lessons, publish articles about education, and help in mentoring new teachers.

Although teachers in mainland China do not earn much, they have opportunities to supplement their salaries by working as tutors or participating in invited talks. In Shanghai and other major cities like Beijing, teaching provides a more steady income than other professions. Thus, it is a preferred occupation. Additionally, teaching in Shanghai is a respected position because the majority of officers in the government education sector begin their careers as teachers (OECD, 2014).

Learning Environment in Shanghai

One factor that allows students to succeed in Shanghai is the high level of student engagement. Teachers do not allow students to be passive. This intense level of engagement results not only from the approach to teaching but also from examination pressure and cultural influence. An OECD (2014) report mentioned research that found students in Shanghai schools to be more engaged than students from other cultures:

> [I]n one typical mathematics lesson observed for this research, students at Junior Secondary II were learning about parabolas. Students covered 15 problems at their desks, and selected students gave blackboard demonstrations. This is rather different from classrooms in other cultures, where students may not be required to be fully engaged or attentive throughout the entire lesson; and the amount of work expected is seldom comparable. (p. 108)

The intense level of student engagement in school persists out of school. Parents expect children to complete homework every day. In Western cultures, on the other hand, schoolwork is less likely to be viewed as something that should interfere with family life. Chinese parents typically do all they can to encourage their children to succeed academically.

Another component of the learning environment in China includes adequate time for students to develop physically and morally. Schools in Shanghai are required to provide students with one hour of physical education on a daily basis. Pupils participate in physical exercise in the morning before school, later during the school day, and after school. Some schools even have their students do eye exercises to prevent eyesight deterioration. Students also have class duties, including cleaning the classrooms and keeping their campus orderly. They even participate in service learning by visiting rural villages or deprived social groups (OECD, 2014).

Children at the elementary level in Shanghai are allowed more time for recess than those at middle schools or high schools. The amount of recess elementary students receive is about 40% of the school day. Across all school levels, a higher percentage of the school day is devoted to recess in Shanghai than in the United States (Chang & Coward, 2015).

Some American schools have reduced recess time to increase academic achievement, but this practice contradicts the research on recess and the strategies that some world-class systems like Shanghai implement to enhance learning. Indeed, research on recess indicates that it enhances learning, classroom management, social development, and physical well-being. Recess supports learning because it permits students to have breaks, which increase energy levels and concentration. When concentration improves, teachers are less likely to have classroom management problems because students are less likely to be disruptive. With regard to social development, recess allows students time to build relationships with one another in an unstructured environment. Finally, recess enhances physical fitness because it allows opportunities for students to move, reducing health problems associated with prolonged sitting that may occur later in life (Chang & Coward, 2015).

Education in Rural Areas of China

While teachers in Shanghai may enjoy favorable conditions, many of their counterparts in rural areas are more likely to endure less desirable circumstances for various reasons. First, in poor areas of rural China, attendance rates are low, as low as 40% at some high schools. Second, school buildings are in poor condition. Third, classrooms tend to contain more students, in some cases as many as 130. In addition, children often work to support their families. These conditions help explain why in previous years policies designed for rural areas, where over 60% of Chinese children live, focused more on school attendance than high test scores. The educational inequalities students in rural areas endure explain why critics object to releasing China's PISA results only from wealthier urban areas like Shanghai. If China were to release average scores from its entire nation, critics believe such scores would likely not be impressive (Loveless, 2013a).

A huge number (260 million) of migrants from rural areas have moved to urban areas in an effort to reap the benefits of China's recent economic boom. Migrant children, however, do not receive the same educational opportunities as children with residency status in urban areas because cities require proof of municipal residence (*hukou*) for students to attend public schools. Consequently, these children must either return to the countryside to live with relatives or attend private schools often inferior in quality. Tom Loveless (2013a) mentioned how the effect of *hukou* is discriminatory, describing how it prevents Chinese families in poor areas from improving their socioeconomic status. He also pointed out that efforts to reform it have been criticized for being ineffective.

One consequence of this situation is that the opportunities for the poor to get a high-quality education have decreased. For example, Peking University, one of the best institutions in China, has experienced lower enrollment of students from rural areas in recent years. Around 30% of students from rural areas attended Peking University in the 1990s, but in the past decade, this percentage fell to 10% (Gao, 2014).

A *New York Times* article mentioned that although the Chinese education system may be viewed as a paradigm for educational equity, this belief does not correspond with the reality:

> China's state education system, which offers nine years of compulsory schooling and admits students to colleges strictly through exam scores, is often hailed abroad as a paradigm for educational equity. The impression is reinforced by Chinese students' consistently stellar performance in international standardized tests. But this reputation is built on a myth.
>
> While China has phenomenally expanded basic education for its people, quadrupling its output of college graduates in the past decade, it has also created a system that discriminates against its less wealthy and well-connected citizens, thwarting social mobility at every step with bureaucratic and financial barriers. (Gao, 2014, paras. 3–4)

Other Inequalities

The reduced opportunities students in rural areas experience are not the only inequalities in the Chinese education system. Students attending schools in cities also endure inequalities because within urban areas, schools vary in quality. Wealthier parents use methods to place their children in better schools that less fortunate pupils cannot attend. For example, some parents spend thousands of dollars in donations to sway top high schools to secure slots for their children. Children from wealthier families also have more opportunities to do well because their parents can invest more on private tutoring, which helps students do well on the college entrance exam. A high score on this exam is needed for future success (Gao, 2014).

Influence of the College Entrance Exam

A discussion of the Chinese educational system would be incomplete without mention of the tremendous impact the *gaokao* has on the lives of Chinese students and parents. This exam is a demanding test given every June over a two- to three-day period. One reason it is a crucial test is that Chinese universities usually use it as the only criterion to admit students. Chinese families believe how well students do on it determines their future. The *gaokao* is the modern version of the *keju*, a test believed to be the first standardized test ever created and used for over 1,000 years to determine men's entry into the civil service (Larmer, 2014).

Another reason the *gaokao* is perceived as a do-or-die test relates to China's unbalanced higher education system. Whereas China's top universities are funded well, the many smaller universities, where immense numbers of students have enrolled in the past two decades, are not. Consequently, these underfunded institutions usually provide poor quality, leading them to be ranked poorly. Mainland China has only two universities in the top 200, according to the *Times Higher Education* world university rankings. Critics believe that such a system fails to prepare many graduates for the labor force. Better higher education systems provide higher quality, allowing more students to have opportunities to get the preparation needed to enter the labor force and lowering the fierce competition to enter a top university (Altbach, 2016).

The *gaokao* is so important that as soon as children start primary school, they compete with one another to get into the schools that will prepare them best for doing well on it. Preparation for this test starts as early as the preschool years because a child who does well in primary school has a better chance of getting into better schools later. Doing well academically in the early years therefore increases a child's chances of being well prepared for the *gaokao*. Consequently, some parents feel pressure to give their children a head start by sending them to tutors as early as during the preschool years. Part of the reason parents provide tutoring this early is that China's kindergarten guidelines, which were updated in 2012, promote the development of well-rounded students and discourage an approach based on developing academic knowledge. Although these guidelines are intended to promote healthy childhood development, parents frequently demand that their children receive rote instruction early in life, believing it will prepare them well for the *gaokao*. As a result, children feel the pressure and stress to do well academically at a very young age. An education institution mentioned that Chinese children experience homework-induced sleep deprivation as early as age three (O'Meara, 2016).

During the time of year when students take the *gaokao*, the atmosphere in China is similar to a national holiday. Everyday activities that may distract students, such as factory and construction work, must stop. Drivers need to use different roads, and police maintain quiet in the streets. It is not unusual to see crowds of parents in cities like Beijing waiting to pick up their children on the last day of the exam. Sometimes students celebrate after completing the exams as their parents give them flower bouquets (Ash, n.d.).

A Stressful Test

Although some students may celebrate when they complete the *gaokao*, which means "big test" in Mandarin, they are under enormous pressure to do well. In addition to sleep deprivation that starts as early as the preschool years, the pressure to do well on the test manifests itself in other ways. Tragic stories appear every year in Chinese newspapers about exam-time suicides, and students take extreme measures to do the best they can. In one district, females reportedly took birth control pills out of fear that their period would distract them (Siegel, 2007).

One school placed fences on its second floor balconies in 2015 to prevent students from jumping to their deaths. The school was responding to two student suicides before the exam, hoping to avoid more tragedies. This school, the Hengshui No. 2 High School, is one of China's best, and it is known for its rigorous academic approach. Students there typically start their day before 6:00 in the morning and study until they go to bed (Phillips, 2015).

An Unfair Admissions Process

The process of being admitted to a university is unfair for many students. Residents of big cities like Beijing and Shanghai have a better chance of getting into an elite university simply because they have resident status at these cities. Universities in cities like Beijing use quotas to admit residents of students in different areas. A resident in Beijing may be admitted with a lower qualifying score than a resident from a rural region because the quota system allows for a higher percentage of students to be admitted from this area. Prestigious universities like Peking University and Tsinghua University need to select much higher percentages of students from Beijing and Shanghai than from other areas like Guangdong.

In some cases, students who have lived their entire lives in a big city need to return to the provinces where they have their residency to take the *gaokao*. This outcome can occur if a family has lived elsewhere before moving to a place like Beijing. Students in this situation may have to not only score higher but also prepare for a different variation of the *gaokao* because the test varies from province to province (Fu, 2013).

This problem is a major concern in China because it affects a large number of students. In 2013, for example, the *Los Angeles Times* reported that according to the municipal education commission, 41% of the students in Beijing's elementary and middle schools did not have official Beijing residency. Further, families object to sending their children to rural provinces because some schools are poorly built. Over 5,000 students were killed in 2008 when schools collapsed during the earthquake in Sichuan (Demick, 2013).

Cultural Attitudes

The importance of the *gaokao* is not the only reason Chinese students study rigorously. Like many other East Asian nations, the Chinese have strong values with respect to education. Their beliefs developed to a great extent from the Confucian philosophy, which originated in China. Part of this philosophy is based on the idea that humans are malleable and capable of improving through personal and communal effort. Consequently, education is valued greatly (OECD, 2014).

To illustrate these strong values, Huabin Chen (2001) conducted a study with over 300 students and parents to explore cultural differences in attitudes and expectations between American and Chinese families. The study found significant differences between the groups with regard to science education:

> The Chinese and American groups significantly differed regarding parents' behavior in helping their children learn science at home. More specifically, the Chinese parents spent more time working with their children, more frequently checked their homework, and bought more books and equipment relating to science for their children than did the American parents. These findings support the conclusions of many previous researchers (Hess et al., 1987; Krum & Astleitner, 1991; Stevenson, Lee, & Stigler, 1986), namely that Chinese parents place greater value on home involvement.... In contrast to American parents, Chinese parents set high standards for their children and

devote much time and energy to helping them, because of the belief that their children can excel (e.g., at science) if they work hard enough. (Chen, 2001, p. 311)

Historical Origins of the Chinese Education System

Some of the educational practices that China implements today originated thousands of years ago. One of these practices is the use of the *gaokao*. As with many of the other chapters in this book, a brief historical perspective will be offered here to better understand how China's education system evolved.

Before and During the Cultural Revolution

The Chinese education system followed the Russian model during the 1950s. This system was rigid. It was based on an ideology that emphasized collectivism. When China's ties with the Soviet Union weakened in the early 1960s, a new approach that emphasized innovation and new ideas emerged.

This trend was short lived as a result of the Cultural Revolution (1966–1976), which devastated China's society and education system. During this period, schools closed and practical learning in farming and factories superseded formal learning. The only people believed to represent the revolutionary ideology were the workers, peasants, and soldiers. Committees consisting of people belonging to these groups took control of schools and higher education (OECD, 2014).

After the Cultural Revolution

After the Cultural Revolution, China had to rebuild its education system. Many reforms were implemented, leading to rapid progress. After being suspended for almost a decade during the revolution, the *gaokao* exams were reinstated in 1977 (Siegel, 2007). Enrollment in basic education increased considerably by the 1990s, and today urban schools at the senior secondary level have high enrollment rates. As mentioned previously, enrollment in higher education has also expanded considerably, but concerns have been raised about the inequalities at this level.

China has also decentralized its education system, allowing authorities at the local level to manage the schools and the school curriculum. However, when decentralization occurred, disparities emerged between urban and rural areas. In response, China implemented policies to alleviate this problem, but inequalities persist.

The nation has also improved teacher quality, training unqualified teachers in rural schools and increasing requirements for teachers at all levels. Shanghai was one of the first areas in the country to have a fully qualified teaching force. This area raised the qualifications for teachers ahead of other parts of the nation (OECD, 2014).

Areas Needing Improvement

Many aspects of China's education system that need improvement relate to the pressure placed on children to do well academically in order to attend a good university. This stress not only leads to the problems previously discussed, such as suicide and sleep deprivation, but also promotes the use of a learning approach based on rote methods of study. In addition, China has problems involving cheating.

Cheating

Because the college entrance exam determines so much of students' futures, the Chinese government puts great effort to guard each year's questions. Those who create the exam do so in a secret location, and the printing occurs in maximum-security prisons. One year, a province spent about $13 million to discourage cheating, installing metal detectors and cameras. Despite facing severe penalties, including banning cheaters from ever taking the *gaokao* again and entering their names in a public database for prospective employers to see, students still cheat (Siegel, 2007).

For example, 54 external invigilators investigated high scores on the *gaokao* exam in the city of Zhongxang in 2013 because students there were disproportionately gaining the limited number of places at China's elite universities. When high school students arrived at one of the schools to take the exam, their mobile phones and secret transmitters were confiscated. At a nearby hotel, a group of officials caught people transmitting answers to the students. A riot occurred when parents came to pick up their children and discovered what had happened. The angry mob starting the riot felt that because cheating is widespread in China, not allowing their children the same advantage as others was unjust (Moore, 2013).

China implemented a law making cheating a crime in 2015 with a maximum punishment of up to seven years in jail. Chinese students and parents have mixed feelings about the new law, with some feeling it is too harsh but others perceiving it as necessary. Although it is too early to know how effective the new law will be, the stronger repercussions will probably not stop cheating completely. Shortly after the new legislation was implemented, 11 educational institutions were shut down in connection with a cheating scheme (Hernandez, 2016).

Rote Methods of Learning

In addition to cheating, the *gaokao* promotes rote methods of teaching that prevent students from thinking in new ways, leading critics to argue that China cannot produce a person like Steve Jobs or Bill Gates. Helen Gao went to schools both in China and the United States and described how the emphasis on rote learning fails to prepare students to be creative:

> When I first came to the U.S. to start school here, after having just finished my junior year at a high school in my native Beijing, I quickly learned that the challenge I faced was more than just a language barrier. The analytical essays on my history tests felt dauntingly, even impossibly amorphous compared to the straightforward multiple-choice questions that had long characterized my exams… I was used to strictly formatted Chinese argumentative essay topics, for which I had memorized hundreds of paragraphs that I could organize like jigsaw puzzles. Western-education-style papers on, for example, the significance of symbols in a novel was not the sort of expressive, creative thinking for which my Chinese teachers had prepared me. (Gao, 2012, para. 5)

The primary purpose of high school in China is to prepare students for the *gaokao*, and the main method to prepare them for this test is through the use of rote learning. In addition, the teacher-centered approach to teaching does not promote discussions but instead repetition and memorization. Teachers rarely pose open-ended questions and do not encourage intellectual curiosity. Instead, they teach according to Confucian values, which emphasize respect for figures of authority, dependence, and harmony. Even university instructors too often fail to teach in a way that promotes problem solving and creativity as they use similar methods to those implemented in high schools (Lucenta, 2011).

Conclusion

China implements few methods that would improve the education system in the United States. Most of the top-performing regions covered in this book create many more opportunities for socioeconomically disadvantaged students to have access to similar educational resources as those coming from wealthier households. However, China provides fewer of these opportunities. Poor rural students typically cannot attend China's superior schools even after they migrate to urban areas. This circumstance occurs as a result of China's *hukou* system, a system that does not permit equal access not only to schools but also to social welfare programs and healthcare providers (Loveless, 2013b).

Further, China's approach to education thwarts creativity, inquiry, and problem solving because students' ultimate goal is to do well on the national college entrance exam. High school teaching is based on rote methods of learning that prepare students for the *gaokao*. Preparing children for this exam starts as early as the preschool years. In addition, the pressure of doing well academically puts students under enormous stress, and suicide rates tend to increase as the time of the *gaokao* approaches (Larmer, 2014).

Shanghai's impressive accomplishments are also misleading. Critics of statistics showing that Shanghai achieved an enrollment rate of over 99% at the age of compulsory education say that this percentage probably does not include migrant children, who account for a considerable portion of its population. Skeptics also question Shanghai's stunning 2009 and 2012 PISA results because Shanghai's scores may represent only the wealthier subset of students who hold Shanghai *hukous* (Loveless, 2013b).

Despite these concerns, educators need to notice the large number of students in China who do well on the PISA. The number of students who do well on this test could be more important than average scores and could possibly be the most important factor to produce leading-edge technology in a global economy (Salzman & Lowell, 2008). In addition, critics who say that China's educational system prevents innovation sometimes overlook China's ability to take advantage of innovations. A recent study showed that China surpassed the United States in research and development that focuses on turning discoveries into commercial products. An article in *USA Today* mentioned that although the United States may be better at inventing new technologies, China is taking advantage of this trend by turning them into commercial products (Davidson, 2017).

China cannot yet be considered one of the leading countries in education because it does not reveal the scores of many provinces where large portions of the population live. Evidence suggests that its poor rural areas contain inferior schools and that inequalities exist in its cities as well. It will be interesting to see if China will release the scores of all its regions in future years. If this is ever done, policymakers will have a more accurate idea of the percentage of China's population that is well educated.

References

Altbach, P. G. (2016, February 19). China's glass ceiling and feet of clay. *University World News*. Retrieved from http://www.universityworldnews.com/article.php?story=20160217143711361

Ash, A. (n.d.). Is China's gaokao the world's toughest school exam? *The Guardian*. Retrieved from https://www.theguardian.com/world/2016/oct/12/gaokao-china-toughest-school-exam-in-world

Chang, R., & Coward, F. L. (2015). More recess time, please! *Phi Delta Kappan, 97*(3), 14–17.

Chen, H. (2001). Parents' attitudes and expectations regarding science education: Comparisons among American, Chinese-American, and Chinese families. *Adolescence, 36*(142), 305–313.

Davidson, P. (2017, April 17). Why China is beating the U.S. at innovation. *USA Today*. Retrieved from https://www.usatoday.com/story/money/2017/04/17/why-china-beating-us-innovation/100016138/

Demick, B. (2013, July 25). Red tape bars many students from China's top colleges. *Los Angeles Times*. Retrieved from http://www.latimes.com/world/la-fg-china-education-discrimination-20130725-dto-htmlstory.html

Fu, Y. (2013, June 19). China's unfair college admissions system. *The Atlantic*. Retrieved from https://www.theatlantic.com/china/archive/2013/06/chinas-unfair-college-admissions-system/276995/

Gao, H. (2012, June 25). The education system that pulled China up may now be holding it back. *The Atlantic*. Retrieved from https://www.theatlantic.com/international/archive/2012/06/the-education-system-that-pulled-china-up-may-now-be-holding-it-back/258787/

Gao, H. (2014, September 4). China's education gap. *The New York Times*. Retrieved from https://www.nytimes.com/2014/09/05/opinion/sunday/chinas-education-gap.html?mcubz=0&_r=0

Hernandez, J. C. (2016). China threatens jail time for college entrance exam cheaters. *The New York Times*. Retrieved from https://www.nytimes.com/2016/06/08/world/asia/china-exam-gaokao-university-cheating.html?mcubz=0

Larmer, B. (2014, December 31). Inside a Chinese test-prep factory. *The New York Times*. Retrieved from https://www.nytimes.com/2015/01/04/magazine/inside-a-chinese-test-prep-factory.html?mcubz=0

Loveless, T. (2013a, October 9). PISA's China problem. *The Brookings Institution*. Retrieved from https://www.brookings.edu/research/pisas-china-problem/

Loveless, T. (2013b, December 11). Attention OECD-PISA: Your silence on China is wrong. *The Brookings Institution*. Retrieved from https://www.brookings.edu/research/attention-oecd-pisa-your-silence-on-china-is-wrong/

Lucenta, L. (2011). China's higher education lacks higher learning. *Phi Delta Kappan, 93*(4), 76–77.

Michael, R. (2016). Education in China. *World Education News & Reviews*. Retrieved from http://wenr.wes.org/2016/03/education-in-china-2

Moore, M. (2013, June 20). Riot after Chinese teachers try to stop pupils cheating. *The Telegraph*. Retrieved from http://www.telegraph.co.uk/news/worldnews/asia/china/10132391/Riot-after-Chinese-teachers-try-to-stop-pupils-cheating.html

O'Meara, S. (2016, August 11). China's high-pressure network of cram-schools for tots. *Foreign Policy*. Retrieved from http://foreignpolicy.com/2016/08/11/chinas-high-pressure-network-of-cram-schools-for-tots/

Organization for Economic Co-operation and Development. (2014). *Strong performers and successful reformers in education: Lessons from PISA for Korea*. Paris: Organization of Economic Cooperation and Development.

Organization for Economic Co-operation and Development. (2016a). *Education in China: A snapshot*. Paris: Organization of Economic Cooperation and Development.

Organization for Economic Co-operation and Development. (2016b). *PISA 2015 high performers: China*. Retrieved from https://www.oecd.org/pisa/PISA-2015-china.pdf

Phillips, T. (2015, April 21). Chinese school installs 'anti-suicide' barriers before dreaded exam. *The Telegraph*. Retrieved from http://www.telegraph.co.uk/news/worldnews/asia/china/11551660/Chinese-school-installs-anti-suicide-barriers-before-dreaded-exam.html

Salzman, H., & Lowell, L. (2008). Making the grade. *Nature, 453*, 28–30.

Siegel, B. (2007, June 12). Stressful times for Chinese students. *Time*. Retrieved from http://content.time.com/time/world/article/0,8599,1631854,00.html

Tucker, M. (2011). Researching other countries' education systems: Why it's indispensible but tricky, how we did it, why this time it's different. In M. Tucker (Ed.), *Surpassing Shanghai: An agenda for American education built on the world's leading systems* (pp. 1–18). Cambridge, MA: Harvard Education Press.

Tucker, M. (2016, December 6). The 2015 PISA results: What do they mean? *Education Week*. Retrieved from http://blogs.edweek.org/edweek/top_performers/2016/12/the_2015_pisa_results_what_do_they_mean.html?r=82450346&print=1

LEARNING FROM CANADA

A Top-Performing Country Similar to the United States

Canada could very well be the most important top-performing country for the United States to borrow ideas from. Several reasons make Canada ideal for this purpose. First, like the United States, Canada is rich in cultural diversity, but many of the other countries covered in this book lack it. In fact, a study conducted for the Harvard Institute of Economic Research rated Canada as more ethnically diverse than the United States (Fisher, 2013). Second, because many of Canada's immigrants came from Europe like those of the United States, its people have cultural attitudes about education that do not differ greatly from its southern neighbor.

Canada's performance on the 2015 PISA was impressive. It ranked highly in all three subjects, coming in 3rd in reading, 10th in math, and 7th in science (Jackson & Kiersz, 2016). Canadian students performed especially well in reading and math, with scores in these subjects well above the OECD averages (O'Grady, Deussing, Scerbina, Fung, & Muhe, 2016).

Canada's success in international testing is recent. This country was not recognized as a leader in international assessments before 2000. However, in the 21st century, Canada has repeatedly performed well on the PISA. More important, this nation has enjoyed success in education in part as a result of the relatively narrow range in performance between its underprivileged students and their more privileged counterparts. OECD mentioned in 2013 that a high percentage of Canadian students from socioeconomically disadvantaged households performed better than would be expected for students with similar backgrounds. This percentage was not only higher than the OECD average but also higher than the United States' average, which usually falls below the OECD average (OECD, 2013). However, Canada is having problems providing equal educational opportunities for its Aboriginal population because the schools students from this group usually attend receive less funding.

Structure of Canada's Educational System

Canada's educational system is different from other top-performing countries because it has no federal department of education. In contrast, each of the 13 jurisdictions is responsible for the organization of its system at the elementary and secondary levels. Although the provinces share similarities, they differ in the policies they implement involving curriculum, assessment, and accountability (Council of Ministers of Education, Canada, n.d.).

Four of Canada's 10 provinces and three territories contain about 80% of the country's five million students. Ontario is the one with the most students (two million). The other three are Quebec (one million), British Columbia (610,000), and Alberta (530,000). Although the country has no national ministry of education, it has the Council of Ministers of Education (CMEC), an organization created to provide the provinces and territories opportunities to work together on initiatives and projects (OECD, 2014).

The provinces and territories have their own ministries or departments, with ministers appointed by the government leader of the jurisdiction. School boards, districts, divisions, or education councils govern at the local level and consist of members elected by public ballot. Because the provinces and boards of education control the education system, the ages for compulsory education vary in different regions; however, most regions require students to enroll from age 6 to age 16. Compulsory education could start at age 5 and end at age 18 (Council of Ministers of Education, Canada, n.d.).

Additionally, control of the educational system is divided between the central provincial government and the locally elected school boards. Although differences in the balance of power between provincial governments and the locally elected school boards may exist, the provincial government typically determines the curriculum, many major school policies, and most or all of the funding. The school boards usually hire staff, principals, and administrators and also control the annual budgets (OECD, 2014).

Teachers' Salaries and Working Hours

Canadian teachers earn a good salary. The average salaries for beginning teachers in 2012/2013 (in U.S. dollars) were $39,660 for both primary and lower secondary levels and $39,826 for the upper secondary level. These salaries were above the OECD averages. In addition, in most of the provinces and territories, teachers receive their maximum salaries after 10 years, much earlier than teachers in other OECD countries (Statistics Canada, 2016).

Canadian teachers normally earn more than teachers in the United States. As a result, qualified candidates are attracted to the profession. Vivien Stewart (2012) compared salaries between a teacher in Edmonton, Alberta, with 11 years of experience and a teacher in Des Moines, Iowa, with similar experience and university education. Although Des Moines is one of the better-paying districts in Iowa, the teacher in Edmonton was earning $81,000 U.S. dollars, but the teacher in Iowa was earning only $49,000 U.S. dollars according to two education associations representing these regions (Stewart, 2012).

However, teachers in Canada generally teach more than their counterparts in other countries. In 2012/2013, for example, teachers at the primary school level taught an average of 795 hours per year, higher than the OECD average of 772 hours. At the lower secondary and upper secondary levels, this trend also occurred (Canadian Education Statistics Council [CESC], 2015).

Teacher Quality

One aspect of Canada's education system that contributes strongly to its success is teacher quality. Like many other top-performing countries in education, Canada chooses its teachers carefully and selects only those in the top 30% of their cohort. Another reason Canada's teachers are well prepared relates to the quality of teacher preparation programs. Canada has considerably fewer teacher preparation programs than the United States, resulting in better training quality and supervision (OECD, 2014).

In comparison, the United States uses lower standards for selecting and preparing teachers:

[I]n the United States, we pay our teachers poorly, content ourselves with very low standards for getting into teachers colleges, prepare them mostly in third tier higher education institutions, don't insist that our teachers really master the subjects they will teach, and take pride in permitting people to teach after only a few weeks or months of crash training in their craft. So we are alarmed when our students fail to compete with their international peers and decide to get tough on our teachers and their unions. (Tucker, 2012, para. 8)

Such a situation leads Canadian students to perceive teacher preparation programs in the United States as having lower admissions requirements than those in their country. Although each Canadian region may have different certification requirements, teachers generally need to have a bachelor's degree and one year of teacher education to teach. Most of the provinces also require candidates to go through a certification process, which may involve taking an exam (National Center on Education and the Economy [NCEE], n.d).

Equitable Funding

Another crucial component of Canada's success in education involves equitable funding. As previously mentioned, Canadian provinces and territories control the majority if not all of the school funding. Their approach to subsidizing schools prevents many of the problems the United States experiences regarding the lack of resources schools in low-income areas receive because the provinces subsidize students in need adequately (Mehta & Schwartz, 2011). However, this trend does not exist with the education of many Canadian Aboriginal students.

In addition to its rich cultural diversity, Canada is one of the most important countries for the United States to model for another reason. Before experiencing its high PISA scores, some of its provinces funded their schools using similar methods to those the United States currently implements. However, Canada experienced outstanding results on international tests only after using more equitable funding practices.

Alberta, for example, had a similar funding system to that of the United States, subsidizing its schools through local taxes and money from the provincial government. A significant amount (40%) from local taxes was used to fund schools, leading poor districts to receive less funding than wealthier areas. However, after the 1994 reforms, this process ended. A new system was implemented that placed the responsibility for the funding entirely on the province. The new system allowed the province to determine the funding level and the distribution. School boards (except for religious boards) no longer received funds through local taxes (Herman, 2013).

Ontario also had a similar system to Alberta's before its reform efforts of 1998. Before reforming, different school boards funded schools inequitably because reliance on local tax revenue led to disparities in programs and services among different parts of the province. After Ontario implemented a school-funding system similar to Alberta's new system, funding to schools was distributed more equitably (Herman, 2013).

In contrast to these funding practices, the United States implements an approach that provides the poor with fewer educational resources than the wealthy. This imbalance in funding occurs because the cost of public school education in the United States is normally funded by property taxes and state grants. The amount received from the grants generally does not balance the inadequate funds poor districts receive from local property taxes, leading to severe inequalities between poor districts and their wealthier counterparts. These inequalities allow wealthier districts to spend considerably more per pupil than the poorer districts (Darling-Hammond, 2014).

Social Policies

The equitable distribution of resources in schools reflects Canada's social policies. Canada's strong national welfare policies allow children and their parents to have access to national health insurance (Mehta & Schwartz, 2011). Although other first-world nations in education have lower child poverty rates than Canada, Canada has a rate lower than the United States. In addition, the United States has a percentage of children living in poverty that has increased from 2008 to 2012, but in 18 countries, this percentage became lower over the same period (Ingraham, 2014). The United States also has more people without health insurance than any other advanced industrial country and offers people with high-paying jobs better benefits than their counterparts with low-paying jobs or no jobs at all. Indeed, the U.S. system does less to alleviate inequality than almost any other rich democracy (Morgan, 2013).

The reason inadequate social policies are significant relates to the problems they contribute to academic achievement. As discussed in Chapter 1, poverty can be more powerful toward impeding academic success than the quality of schools and teachers. David Berliner (2009) argued that harsh social policies, like those of the United States, and the poverty they promote are more responsible for the academic achievement gap that exists in the United States than poor teaching or school quality. Canada is much less likely to implement harsh social policies because the concept of social welfare is more ingrained there than in the United States. This ideal manifests itself in Canada's strong welfare system and equitable schools. In the United States, on the other hand, the poor social policies and the inequalities in schools reflect the country's individualistic ideals (Mehta & Schwartz, 2011).

The Education of Immigrants

Because Canada has one of the highest rates of immigration in the world, it could not have experienced its success in education without providing adequate resources for immigrant children to perform well academically. The PISA results show that Canadian immigrants do indeed perform better than immigrants in other countries and reflect Canada's commitment to educate members of its immigrant communities. For example, Canadian first generation immigrants achieved an average score that was over 510 in reading on the 2003 PISA, higher than the United States' score for this group. Whereas other countries, including the United States and Germany experience an achievement gap between their native and immigrant students on the PISA, no such gap exists in Canada. In addition, students who speak a different language at home than the language of instruction do just as well academically as those not speaking a different language at home (Mehta & Schwartz, 2011). However, significant differences exist in the academic achievement of different immigrants. For example, one report found that only 36% of second-generation immigrants from the Caribbean and Central and South America pursue university studies by the age of 21 but that over 80% of those from Africa or China do so (Bothwell, 2015).

Three types of immigrant groups are admitted to Canada for permanent residence. Refugees are admitted for humanitarian reasons. A second group is allowed to come to be reunited with family members, and the third group is admitted because they have the skills and education needed to enhance Canada's economic development and prosperity. Although Canada has a commitment to admit immigrants for family reunification and humanitarian reasons, the country has focused more on admitting newcomers for economic reasons in the 21st century. In 2007, for example, economic immigrants constituted 55.4% of all immigrant admittance, while those admitted for family reunification (28.0%) and for humanitarian (11.8%) reasons comprised a smaller percentage. The preference for admitting immigrants for economic reasons became noticeable in the late 1980s. By 2001, a very high proportion of economic immigrants were admitted (King, 2009).

One reason that immigrant students do well academically has to do with the country's recent success with ESL (English as a second language) students. For example, only 24% of ESL students in Ontario were making progress in 2003, but 10 years later, a remarkable 73% were either meeting or exceeding provincial standards and doing well on international tests like TIMMS and PISA (Howe, 2014).

Another reason immigrant students do better in Canada than in most nations relates to the strong level of education their parents have achieved. Those who endure academic problems frequently come as a result of unfavorable circumstances in their native country. In addition to the difficult process of transitioning to a new school system, students who endure traumatic events, such as war, in their native country face additional barriers that may impede their academic success. For example, a study on late-adolescent immigrant students coming from war-zone regions found that although the students experienced high levels of academic engagement and motivation, they needed longer times to complete high school than youth entering Canada from countries without military conflicts (Stermac, Elgie, Clarke, & Dunlap, 2012).

Multiculturalism

Canada's effort to promote the academic success of its immigrant students reflects the country's commitment to multiculturalism. Schools assign most immigrant students to classes with non-immigrant students. Furthermore, some of the provinces have a policy designed especially to encourage the success of these students. For example, British Columbia subsidizes language support for students who meet certain criteria. Further, Canada generally has a respectful attitude toward their immigrant population because it views this group as a necessary component of the country's economic growth. For these reasons, Canada is usually viewed as a nation with a welcoming attitude toward immigrants (Mehta & Schwartz, 2011).

Despite Canada's attempts to treat its immigrant communities well, concerns have been raised in the 21st century about the extent to which schools have been able to cope with the country's increasing diversity. Racism and persistent stereotyping have been reported in some schools. Some second-generation immigrant youth, for example, have experienced daily racism, leading some scholars to question whether multiculturalism can provide adequate protection against this type of treatment (Kirova, 2008).

Two Notable Regions

In addition to exploring the entire country's approach to education and some of Canada's challenges, examining the regions that do best in international testing can provide insights on particular methods Canada implements that may benefit the United States. Two notable areas known for their success on the PISA are Alberta and Ontario.

Alberta

Alberta was at one point the highest-scoring province on the PISA, achieving this success in part as a result of its high quality curriculum (OECD, 2014). This province is about the size of Iowa, with a student population similar to Iowa's. Although Iowa and Alberta have a comparable percentage of students at the poverty level, students in Alberta generally achieve higher scores on international tests (Stewart, 2012).

Alberta's curriculum is a high-quality curriculum for several reasons. First, teachers participated in developing and assessing it. Second, every student receives a strong academic foundation because all schools in the province are expected to follow the curriculum. Third, it covers all subjects, not just math and reading. Finally, it is much more detailed than the curriculum guidelines used by many U.S. states before the Common Core State Standards were implemented. Alberta's curriculum is believed to have contributed to students' strong results in 2006 on the PISA science test. On this test, 18.4% of students in Alberta scored at the very top, with only 6.1% scoring at the lowest level. In comparison, only 9% of U.S. students scored at the very top, with 24% scoring at the very bottom (Stewart, 2012).

Since the 2006 PISA, the United States has made progress with respect to implementing a curriculum similar to Alberta's by creating the Common Core State Standards, which have been adopted by over 40 states. One reason Alberta's curriculum is believed to promote high PISA scores is that it is implemented in the entire province, leading to consistency across the region.

In the United States, on the other hand, before the Common Core State Standards were created, consistency among the states regarding the rigor of the standards was a problem. Massachusetts, for example, had higher academic standards than Tennessee (Bidwell, 2014).

Another aspect of Alberta's approach to education worthy of mention is the Alberta School Improvement Scheme. This program allows teachers to present innovations involving student engagement and teaching practices. It also includes an annual conference where professionals present and share their findings. This approach enhances teachers' attitudes toward research and improves their skills in using data (Stewart, 2012).

Ontario

Ontario is another region that deserves attention for its recent remarkable gains in education:

> Between 2003 and 2010, Ontario was a world leader in its sustained strategy of professionally-driven education reform. Initiated by Premier Dalton McGuinty on his election in 2003, the Ontario strategy has achieved widespread positive results in increasing elementary literacy and numeracy, improving graduation rates, and reducing the number of low-performing schools. (OECD, 2014, p. 156)

As the largest and most populated province in Canada, Ontario is where about 40% of all Canadians live. It consists of an area of approximately 1,100,000 square kilometers and contributes about 37% of the country's GDP. Its major city is Toronto, one of the world's most diverse cities. To fulfill Canada's requirements for public support of religious minorities and minority languages, Ontario has four sets of locally elected school boards. They consist of 31 English public boards, 29 English Catholic boards, 8 French Catholic boards, and 4 French public boards (OECD, 2014).

Ontario is important for American policymakers to explore because 25 years ago, this region experienced many of the problems the United States currently endures. However, after Dalton McGuinty was elected early in the 21st century, new methods were implemented that dramatically improved the education system.

The problems involving Ontario's educational system in the 1990s included poor teacher morale, public skepticism, and several years of teacher strikes. These outcomes occurred in part because the government's education policies were not popular with teachers. The government had reduced professional development, cut funding, and even blamed teachers for poor results through television ads. However, when Dalton McGuinty headed a new government, the approach to education changed. The government worked with teachers, using their input for ideas on effective reform. This approach restored trust because the methods teachers disapproved of, such as teacher testing, were discontinued as more professional development was added to enhance student improvement and teacher quality (Stewart, 2012).

When McGuinty was elected, he had two goals: to increase high school graduation rates and literacy and numeracy skills at the elementary level. In addition, the government aimed to increase the number of students achieving at the provincial standard in reading, writing, and math. The ministry focused on improving all schools and devoted special attention to the lowest-performing schools. Rather than blame teachers for poor results, the new approach focused on providing struggling schools with additional resources. The signing of an important four-year collective bargaining agreement in 2005 alleviated the previous friction between the teachers' unions and the government, creating more opportunities to focus on school improvement. The agreement addressed the concerns of teachers, allowing the government's strategy for progress to move forward smoothly. The goal of improving literacy and numeracy skills was fulfilled as the proportion of students meeting the provincial standards went up significantly in reading, mathematics, and writing at the third and sixth grade levels. High school graduation rates also increased (OECD, 2014).

One reason that Ontario's reforms were successful involved consulting with school personnel and avoiding a top-down approach of reform. Instead of choosing bureaucrats to lead the reforms, the ministry selected educators to work on numeracy and literacy initiatives. Schools created teams to set goals and plan how to meet them. Teachers were provided with professional development on important instructional practices and were offered more time for professional learning. To lower dropout rates, school personnel looked for data to identify students more likely to dropout and used this information to implement programs to keep these students engaged. Funding was also provided to each district to hire a leader who would promote student success (Stewart, 2012).

Another reason for Ontario's educational success involved its efforts in educating teachers about social justice issues. Because Ontario has a high percentage of immigrant students, the region has a strong commitment to implementing equitable practices that require educators to be knowledgeable about this topic. Consequently, the Ontario Institute for Studies in Education of the

University of Toronto created programs that deal with social justice, human rights, equity, and race. Teacher candidates can enroll in a program that offers opportunities to focus on Aboriginal education or in one that emphasizes social justice issues in education. Although no separate courses deal entirely with these topics, some of them cover these issues. For example, one course that all BEd (Bachelor of Education) students are required to take that covers topics involving equity is called School and Society (Howe, 2014).

Ontario's strategy of reform differs in several ways from the methods that have been implemented in the 21st century in the United States:

> Missing from the strategy are elements that are common in a number of other reform efforts, particularly in the United States: punitive accountability, performance pay, and competition among schools....This means that the key ideas are less about "hard" concepts like accountability and incentives and more about "softer" ideas like culture, leadership, and shared purpose. There is also little emphasis in the Ontario strategy on "getting better people"; rather, the idea is that you have to work with what you have and work to upgrade their skills. In all of these respects, the Ontario model challenges more market-based theories of reform. (Mehta & Schwartz, 2011, p. 158)

Rather than close schools and fire teachers as the United States did in the 21st century, Ontario used appropriate intervention and support. It reduced the number of low-performing schools by providing the technical assistance needed for improvement. This approach reflects trust in teachers. In implementing such a strategy, policymakers generally assume that teachers want to produce good results but may fail to do so because they simply lack knowledge (Mehta & Schwartz, 2011).

Aboriginal Canadians

Although the Canadian educational system currently makes an effort to promote equity for most of the population, Aboriginal students in Canada do not perform as well academically as other groups and experience high levels of inequality. A recent study supports Canada's reputation as a world leader in equity between immigrant and non-immigrant groups but points to the growing academic achievement gap between the Aboriginal groups and the rest of the population. Research from the Environics Institute found that although the percentage of the Aboriginal population between the ages of 25 and 54 with a university degree went up by 2% from 2006 to 2011, the educational attainment of non-Aboriginal Canadians increased at a faster rate (Bothwell, 2015).

Aboriginal people in Canada consist of three groups: First Nations, Metis, and Inuit. These groups constitute about 4% of the population, each having its own language and culture. Members of these groups tend to be younger than other Canadians. In addition to concerns about how the academic achievement gap between Aboriginals and non-Aboriginals may be increasing are concerns about how wide this gap is. It is estimated that non-Aboriginal Canadians complete high school at almost twice the rate of Aboriginals (Edgerton, Roberts, & Eliasova, 2016).

The problems that the Aboriginal people endure can be best understood from a historical perspective. Family dysfunction is believed to be linked to the ways Aboriginal communities were mistreated for many generations during the residential school program, which involved removing Aboriginal children by force and placing them in religious schools. This practice was declared to meet the definition of "cultural genocide" by the Truth and Reconciliation Commission, a Canadian government-appointed organization. Conditions at the residential schools were brutal and led to the death of over 5,000 children. Children at these schools suffered from malnutrition, disease, and physical abuse (Bronski, 2016).

Another problem the Aboriginal communities currently face is a high suicide rate. A First Nations leader connected the suicide problem to childhood sexual abuse, a problem believed to be rampant in Aboriginal communities and linked to the horrific conditions at the residential schools. Aboriginal leaders say that church staff and clergy molested children at these schools, leading to a vicious cycle of sexual abuse that has persisted for generations (Chin, 2017). Aboriginal youth die of suicide at a rate five to six times higher than non-Aboriginals. They, along with Aboriginal adults younger than 44 years of age, die more often from suicide than from any other cause. It is not unusual for 10-year-old children from First Nations families to die of suicide (Bronski, 2016).

Although most of the Canadian population may be reaping the benefits of an adequate welfare system, Aboriginal communities are not receiving the support they need. Consequently, their average life spans are lower than the national average, and some communities endure very high rates of tuberculosis. On some Canadian reservations where they live, HIV and AIDS rates have been reported to be higher than the African countries most susceptible to these conditions. Although Canada has a reputation for funding its schools equitably, the federally funded schools on Aboriginal reservations are poorly subsidized, receiving an average of only 70% of the funds other Canadian schools receive. The lack of educational opportunities and high child poverty rates (over half of children live in poverty) that Aboriginal children endure contribute to low high school graduation rates on reservations. Homes on reservations are overcrowded and require repairs. The horrible living conditions, high poverty rates, and lack of educational opportunities lead to incarceration levels nine times higher than the national average. Twenty-five percent of prisoners in Canada's federal prisons consist of people with Aboriginal ancestry, even though they constitute only 4% of the population. Further, Aboriginals not living on reservations also withstand the devastating effects of poverty. Although half of the Aboriginal people live in urban centers, they experience Canada's second highest unemployment rates. The group with the highest unemployment rates consists of the Aboriginals who live on the reservations (Bronski, 2016).

Areas Needing Improvement

The history of the Aboriginals in Canada as a colonized group is a tragic aspect of this nation's past. Although their previous mistreatment cannot be changed, more needs to be done to alleviate the inequalities they currently experience. Jane Preston (2016) indicated that although positive changes have been made, vast improvement is needed pertaining to the education of Aboriginal people. She identified four crucial components of education that need improvement for Canadian Aboriginal groups to make more progress through education: early childhood education, Aboriginal pedagogy, postsecondary education, and governance and partnerships.

A crucial component for progress involves having an understanding of the Aboriginal worldview. Aboriginal groups view the world with respect for individual people and for differences in culture and belief systems. They perceive all living and nonliving things as interconnected. Rivers, earth, plants, and animals all have spirit (Preston, 2016).

Because Aboriginal communities receive less funding than other Canadian groups, increasing subsidies is critical:

> Through policy, action, and ethically safe conversations, bureaucratic agencies need to recognize the contextualized realities of Aboriginal communities.... [F]unding must be supplied to Aboriginal students in pursuit of early childhood to postsecondary education. At a local level, school boards must assume greater responsibility for promoting early childhood education within their schools. At provincial and federal levels, postsecondary institutions must prioritize the education of Aboriginal peoples. Such commitment entails increased funding for incorporating and staffing Aboriginal programs and content within all levels of education. (Preston, 2016, p. 23)

Other challenges that some Canadian provinces face include lowering high dropout rates and creating universal education. Although the aforementioned comparisons between Iowa and Alberta showed that Alberta's students achieved higher scores on the 2006 PISA than their American counterparts, Alberta also had higher dropout rates than Iowa. In addition, although Ontario made remarkable progress in education in the 21st century, it still has not achieved universal high school graduation (Stewart, 2012).

Conclusion

American policymakers can probably implement more methods from the Canadian educational system with success than from any other country's system because Canada is more similar to the United States than any other top-performing country in education. For example, although Finland has an outstanding education system, borrowing ideas from Finland may be more difficult than using Canada for this purpose because Finland has a homogenous population. In addition, implementing methods that originate in Asian nations is challenging due to cultural attitudes that differ greatly between the East and the West. Most of the East Asian top-performers also have homogenous populations, unlike the United States. In contrast to many other top-performing educational systems, Canada has a very diverse population and also a similar history to the United States.

One of the most important practices Canada implemented to achieve its recognition as a world leader in education involves the equitable funding of its schools. Before eliminating inequitable funding practices similar to the kinds the United States currently practices, Canada was not a world leader in education. Instead of being funded equitably, many Canadian schools received a significant portion of their subsidies from local property taxes, leading to similar inequalities that schools in the United States currently endure. Ending this practice helped Canada improve its schools, but inequalities still persist with regard to the way schools in Aboriginal communities are funded.

Another noteworthy method of reform Canada implemented occurred in Ontario. In this region, rather than get rid of teachers or use punitive approaches of reform, the ministry consulted with schools, implementing a bottom-up approach that created more opportunities for professional development and technical assistance. This approach worked as high school graduation rates and academic skills in literacy and math improved. In addition,

Canada is much more selective than the United States in admitting teacher candidates to teacher preparation programs, choosing only those in the top 30% of their cohort (OECD, 2014).

Unfortunately, as a result of a tragic past, Canadian Aboriginal groups still suffer considerably and endure poor treatment. For over a hundred years, Aboriginal children attended over 130 residential schools usually by force. These schools date back to the 1870s, with the last one closing in 1996. Children were prevented from speaking their language or practicing their culture, leading to social problems that have persisted until today (Truth and Reconciliation Commission of Canada, n.d.). Some of these problems include high suicide rates and family dysfunction.

Aboriginal communities continue to be mistreated today in part because of poor educational opportunities. Unlike most schools in Canada, significant differences in funding exist between Aboriginal schools and non-Aboriginal schools. For example, funding for First Nations schools from kindergarten to the 12th grade is 30% less than funding for other schools (Preston, 2016).

Although Canada is still struggling to correct the problems its Aboriginal communities experience in schools and society, it has made tremendous progress with other groups, helping the country to be recognized as one with a world-class education system. While immigrants generally do as well academically as non-immigrants, certain immigrant groups have more problems than others. Young Filipinos in Canada, for example, often fail to meet or exceed their parents' academic achievements and tend to do less well academically than other immigrant groups (Farrales, 2017).

The methods Canada implemented to reform its school system in the past 25 years could easily be applied in the United States. These reforms would likely enhance the American system dramatically. The problems that the Canadian Aboriginal communities endure can help American policymakers think of ways to better treat the Aboriginal groups in the United States.

References

Berliner, D. (2009). Are teachers responsible for low achievement by poor students? *Kappa Delta Pi Record*, 46(1), 18–21.

Bidwell, A. (2014, February 27). The history of Common Core State Standards. *U.S. News and World Report*. Retrieved from https://www.usnews.com/news/special-reports/articles/2014/02/27/the-history-of-common-core-state-standards

Bothwell, E. (2015, September 16). Gap between education of aboriginal and non-aboriginal people in Canada widening. *Times Higher Education*. Retrieved from https://www.timeshighereducation.com/news/gap-between-education-aboriginal-and-non-aboriginal-people-canada-widening

Bronski, C. (2016, March 18). Manitoba aboriginal youth suicides exemplify systemic crisis. *International Committee of the Fourth International*. Retrieved from https://www.wsws.org/en/articles/2016/03/18/cana-m18.html

Canadian Education Statistics Council. (2015). *Education indicators in Canada: An international perspective 2015*. Retrieved from http://www.statcan.gc.ca/pub/81-604-x/81-604-x2015001-eng.pdf

Chin, J. (2017, January 13). Indigenous youth suicide crisis solution is "not rocket science": Angus. *The Huffington Post*. Retrieved from http://www.huffingtonpost.ca/2017/01/13/first-nations-suicide-crisis_n_14155122.html

Council of Ministers of Education, Canada. (n.d.). *Education in Canada: An overview*. Retrieved from http://www.cmec.ca/299/Education-in-Canada-An-Overview/

Darling-Hammond, L. (2014). What can PISA tell us about U.S. education policy? *New England Journal of Public Policy, 26*(1), 1–14.

Edgerton, J. D., Roberts, L. W., & Eliasova, V. (2016). Education in Canada: Separate but similar systems in the pursuit of excellence and equity. In H. Morgan & C. Barry (Eds.), *The world leaders in education: Lessons from the successes and drawbacks of their methods* (pp. 79–106). New York, NY: Peter Lang Publishing.

Farrales, M. (2017). Delayed, deferred and dropped out: Geographies of Filipino-Canadian high school students. *Children's Geographies, 15*(2), 207–223.

Fisher, M. (2013, May 16). A revealing map of the world's most and least ethnically diverse countries. *The Washington Post*. Retrieved from https://www.washingtonpost.com/news/worldviews/wp/2013/05/16/a-revealing-map-of-the-worlds-most-and-least-ethnically-diverse-countries/?utm_term=.4a6afb65e914

Herman, J. (2013). *Canada's approach to school funding: The adoption of provincial control of education funding in three provinces*. Washington, DC: Center for American Progress.

Howe, E. R. (2014). A narrative of teacher education in Canada: Multiculturalism, technology, bridging theory and practice. *Journal of Education for Teaching, 40*(5), 588–599.

Ingraham, C. (2014, October 29). Child poverty in the U.S. is among the worst in the developed world. *The Washington Post*. Retrieved from https://www.washingtonpost.com/news/wonk/wp/2014/10/29/child-poverty-in-the-u-s-is-among-the-worst-in-the-developed-world/?utm_term=.ad8fa00fb0c2

Jackson, A., & Kiersz, A. (2016). The latest ranking of top countries in math, reading, and science is out—and the US didn't crack the top 10. *Business Insider*. Retrieved from http://www.businessinsider.com/pisa-worldwide-ranking-of-math-science-reading-skills-2016-12

King, K. M. (2009). *The geography of immigration in Canada: Settlement, education, labour activity and occupation profiles*. Toronto, ON: Martin Prosperity Institute.

Kirova, A. (2008). Critical and emerging discourses in multicultural education literature: A review. *Canadian Ethnic Studies, 40*(1), 101–124.

Mehta, J. D., & Schwartz, R. B. (2011). Canada: Looks a lot like us but gets much better results. In M. Tucker (Ed.), *Surpassing Shanghai: An agenda for American education built on the world's leading systems* (pp. 141–163). Cambridge, MA: Harvard Education Press.

Morgan, K. J. (2013). America's misguided approach to social welfare: How the country could get more for less. *Foreign Affairs*. Retrieved from ttps://www.foreignaffairs.com/articles/united-states/2012-12-03/americas-misguided-approach-social-welfare

National Center on Education and the Economy. (n.d.). *Canada: Teacher and principal quality*. Retrieved from http://ncee.org/what-we-do/center-on-international-education-benchmarking/top-performing-countries/canada-overview/canada-teacher-and-principal-quality/

O'Grady, K., Deussing, M., Scerbina, T., Fung, K., & Muhe, N. (2016). *Measuring up: Canadian results of the OECD PISA study*. Toronto, ON: Council of Ministers of Education.

Organization for Economic Co-operation and Development. (2013). *PISA 2012 Results: Excellence through equity: Giving every student the chance to succeed* (Vol. II). Paris: Organization of Economic Cooperation and Development.

Organization for Economic Co-operation and Development. (2014). *Strong performers and successful reformers in education: Lessons from PISA for Korea*. Paris: Organization of Economic Cooperation and Development.

Preston, J. P. (2016). Education for Aboriginal peoples in Canada: An overview of four realms of success. *Diaspora, Indigenous, and Minority Education, 10*(1), 14–27.

Statistics Canada. (2016). *Chapter A: The output of educational institutions and the impact of learning*. Retrieved from http://www.statcan.gc.ca/pub/81-604-x/2015001/hl-fs-eng.htm

Stermac, L., Elgie, S., Clarke, A., & Dunlap, H. (2012). Academic experiences of war-zone students in Canada. *Journal of Youth Studies, 15*(3), 311–328.

Stewart, V. (2012). *A world-class education: Learning from international models of excellence and innovation*. Alexandria, VA: ASCD.

Truth and Reconciliation Commission of Canada. (n.d.). *Residential schools*. Retrieved from http://www.trc.ca/websites/trcinstitution/index.php?p=4

Tucker, M. (2012, January 5). An international perspective on teacher quality. *Education Week*. Retrieved from http://blogs.edweek.org/edweek/top_performers/2012/01/an_international_perspective_on_teacher_quality.html

· 8 ·

ESTONIA

A New World Leader in International Testing

Estonia has recently gained the attention of educators for its impressive performance on the PISA. This nation has a high-performing educational system with almost universal participation in schooling, leading its secondary level students to perform among the best in Europe in international assessments in recent years (Santiago, Levitas, Radó, & Shewbridge, 2016). On the PISA 2015 assessment, for example, Estonian students ranked 9th in math, 6th in reading, and 3rd in science (Jackson & Kiersz, 2016).

Although Estonia has not received as much attention as the other countries mentioned in this book, this lack of recognition could change soon if its students continue to improve or maintain their impressive PISA scores. In addition to scoring highly, Estonia's students made other remarkable achievements. For example, Estonia was recently recognized as having the lowest percentage of poor-performing students in math, reading, and science in all of Europe (Butrymowicz, 2016).

How did Estonia achieve these remarkable results? Like many other top-performing nations in education, Estonia created a school system that allowed students from different backgrounds to receive high-quality instruction:

Though its students may come from diverse backgrounds, Estonia's schools give them very similar educational experiences. In embracing students of all backgrounds and income levels, Estonia has succeeded not only on exams but on a goal that many policymakers, educators, and advocates say the United States must achieve: creating an educational system based on equity. (Butrymowicz, 2016, para. 7)

Overview of Estonia

Estonia is one of three Baltic countries along with Lithuania and Latvia. It became independent in 1991 after the collapse of the Soviet Union. The government, parliament, and Ministry of Education and Research control the country's education policy. Although the major language is Estonian, ethnic minority students, such as Russians, have access to bilingual education. Compulsory education starts at age 7 and ends at age 16, and the academic year runs from September to June (EP-Nuffic, 2015).

The Estonian economy has expanded considerably in the past 25 years, gaining recognition as an advanced economy by the International Monetary Fund (IMF). A strong factor of Estonia's economic success involves its information technology sector, which would not have grown without an educational system designed to support the technology skills needed for a high-wage economy. Estonia's economic success is therefore linked to its educational system. The country's economic progress did not occur by chance. In 1998, one of Estonia's strategies was to develop progress in technology by 2015 through a project designed to integrate computer science teaching at the secondary level (Delaney & Kraemer, n.d.).

Equity

Estonia's economic success is a result not only of an education system that supports the technology skills needed for a high-wage economy but also of a system based on equity. Socioeconomic background has less of an effect toward the educational opportunities available for students in Estonia than the effect it has on students in many other OECD countries:

> Estonia has also a good record in promoting equity in schools. The capacity of Estonian schools to compensate for the negative impact of low socio-economic status on learning is high in international comparison. According to PISA, students' socio-economic background has a smaller impact on performance in Estonia than [the impact it has] in other OECD countries. (Santiago et al., 2016, p. 78)

As previously mentioned, Estonia has fewer low-performing students than other nations. A recent study concluded that a very small percentage of the difference in mathematics performance in Estonia could be explained by variations in educational opportunities. As a consequence of Estonia's commitment to equity, 48% of socioeconomically disadvantaged students achieve at the highest levels on PISA, the 6th highest rate in the world (National Center on Education and the Economy [NCEE], n.d.-a).

Some of the ways the education system promotes equality involve the even distribution of qualified teachers and resources. For example, the percentage of teachers with five years of teaching experience does not vary significantly between schools where larger and smaller numbers of low-income students attend (Santiago et al., 2016). With regard to the general access to educational resources, an OECD (2013) report mentioned that Estonia was one of five countries where principals in low-income schools were likely to state that their schools had as many educational resources as schools with higher percentages of privileged students.

Teacher Recruitment and Pay

Although Estonia's educational system has been crucial in helping the country improve its economic status, it differs from many other high-performing nations with regard to teacher recruitment and teacher pay. These differences may surprise policymakers because they are antithetical to the methods other top-performing systems use to achieve stellar results. For example, whereas most world-class nations in education select only the top students in the country to enter the teaching profession, Estonia selects the majority of its candidates from the lower half of university applicants. Another difference that may be surprising involves teachers' pay. Although most teachers in top-performing nations earn a decent salary, teachers in Estonia earn a salary that is rather low (National Center on Education and the Economy [NCEE], n.d.-b).

The Estonian government did make an effort to raise teacher pay. Between 2005 and 2012, experienced lower secondary teachers received a salary increase of 30%. During these years, this increase was the highest in OECD countries. Increases also occurred in 2013 and 2014 when teachers' minimum salaries went up by 11% and then 11.8%. Despite these efforts, teacher salaries remain low when compared with those of other Estonian workers with similar education levels. Preschool and lower secondary teachers in Estonia make 61% and 84% of the average salary of tertiary-educated workers. These percentages are below the OECD averages of 80% and 88% (Santiago et al., 2016).

Teacher Training

Although teachers in Estonia make less than the OECD average, the Estonian government has made teacher-training programs attractive to promising candidates by offering scholarships in the amount of 160 EUR per month. A five-year master's degree is required for teachers at the basic and upper secondary levels, but this requirement does not apply to teachers of elective subjects, allowing them to teach with either a bachelor's or a master's degree. Preschool teachers in Estonia are required to complete a bachelor's degree that can normally be completed in three years. Nearly 93% of general education teachers had a master's level degree in 2013. Although students are generally admitted to these programs according to the same rules used for other programs in higher education, teacher candidates often participate in an interview (Santiago et al., 2016).

Teacher education in Estonia prepares teachers to teach various subjects using research-based methods. Teacher candidates also learn how to design curriculum, differentiate instruction, and motivate students. In addition, they gain an understanding of Estonia's professional standards. Teacher training consists of several stages, including pre-service education and an induction year. During pre-service education, students develop the knowledge and skills needed to teach. During the induction year, novice teachers develop their skills at educational institutions. At this stage, they work with mentor teachers. If they complete this stage successfully, they receive a certificate of teaching from a certification board (Delaney & Kraemer, n.d.).

Teachers continue to enhance their skills and knowledge through professional development after they get hired to work for a school. Various organizations provide this form of training in Estonia, including teachers' professional organizations, teacher education institutions, and private companies. Teachers get professional development free of charge. In previous years, they were required to take 160 hours of professional development every five years. Currently, this system is being changed so that teachers can choose the professional activities they take. Although teachers have choice, their supervisors offer guidance and may recommend certain professional development activities (Santiago et al., 2016).

Career Enhancement

Estonia offers opportunities for teachers to enhance their careers by allowing them chances to take on roles requiring more and varying responsibilities. Before 2013, the career structure was based on four stages: junior teacher, teacher, senior teacher, and teacher methodologist. In 2013, a new system was introduced based on the following four levels:

- **Teacher (level 6):** This level applies to preschool teachers when they enter the teaching profession. This level is awarded indefinitely.
- **Teacher (level 7.1):** This is the level that applies to primary and secondary teachers when they enter the teaching profession. This level is also awarded indefinitely.
- **Senior Teacher (level 7.2):** This level is offered to teachers who teach and also support other teachers and the progress of the school. This level is awarded for five years, but teachers can reapply to remain at this level.
- **Master Teacher (level 8):** This level is offered to teachers who teach, engage in creative activities at their school, and work with a higher education institution. Like the senior teacher level, this one is also awarded for five years, but teachers can reapply to remain at this level.

Teachers specializing in vocational education have a career structure based on different professional standards. These teachers can work at three levels based on their experience and professional competencies:

- **Level 5 Vocational Teacher:** This level applies to teachers who help students develop practical skills.
- **Level 6 Vocational Teacher:** In addition to performing the work of teachers at level 5, teachers at this level work with professional associations and companies.
- **Level 7 Vocational Teacher:** In addition to performing the work of teachers at levels 5 and 6, teachers at this level mentor and supervise other teachers and contribute to the development and reputation of vocational education.

The process of enhancing one's teaching career is a competency-based process. For teachers to move up in rank, they need to have the competencies needed to perform at a higher stage. Professional standards are used as a reference to determine if teachers have the needed competencies. This approach is beneficial because it is linked to practice (Santiago et al., 2016).

Before using this process, Estonia used the teacher attestation model, a model that focused on academic knowledge rather than professional standards. This model was less connected to teachers' core work. One of the advantages of the new model is that it creates greater career diversification. As teachers gain more skills involving teaching, curriculum, assessment, and mentoring, they acquire the qualifications needed to fulfill new positions. Another advantage of the new model is that it encourages experienced teachers to provide guidance to beginning teachers through a 12-month mentoring program, allowing them a chance to move up by helping novice teachers. Although the new model is better than the previous one, Estonian induction programs need improvement:

> 58.6% of Estonian lower secondary teachers were in schools where the principal reported that no formal induction programme was available for new teachers, compared to the international average of 34.2%; and 88% reportedly were in schools with informal induction activities, compared to 77% internationally[.] (Santiago et al., 2016, p. 208)

Structure of the School System

In addition to good professional development practices, effective teacher education programs, and opportunities to move up the career ladder, other aspects of Estonia's schools system contribute to this country's success in education. Some of these components involve the structure of its school system, including the policies on preschool education, basic education, upper secondary education, special education, and vocational education (Santiago et al., 2016).

Preschool Education

Estonian municipalities are responsible for providing and financing preschool education. According to Estonia's Preschool Child Care Institutions Act, all children between the ages of 1.5 and 7 years have the right to receive preschool education. However, some municipalities have not been able to provide it for all children. Consequently, enrollment of children in private preschools has increased in recent years. In addition, Estonia has experienced an increase in the overall number of students enrolled at this level. From 2005 to 2014, for example, preschool institutions experienced an increase in enrollment of 25.9%. In comparison with most OECD countries, Estonia has a higher percentage of students enrolled at this level. Whereas the OECD averages for preschool enrollment in 2012 for ages 3, 4, and 5 were 70%, 84%, and 94%, Estonia's rates for the same year were 89%, 91%, and 91% (Santiago et al., 2016).

Preschools are designed to develop children's social, personal, learning, and play skills. Although children are generally taught in Estonian, they are sometimes taught in different languages at the discretion of the local government council. Starting at age 3, children whose native language is not Estonian are taught Estonian as a second language. Teaching and learning at this level correspond to the national curriculum for preschool child care institutions, a curriculum based on various child-centered approaches of learning including the Montessori and the Waldorf methods. In addition to implementing a learning style that focuses on individuality and creativity, educators focus on teaching values and creating an environment that supports children's safety through an approach that prevents bullying and develops tolerance, honesty, and courage (Ministry of Education and Research, 2014a).

Special education services are guaranteed at the preschool level. It was estimated in 2012 that about 11% of children in Estonia at the preschool level had special needs. These children receive special education services in part through state supported speech therapists and special education teachers. These kinds of services and the child-centered approach contribute to the favorable descriptions about Estonia's preschool programs that international studies often include. While such services are guaranteed, they are not completely free. Parents pay an amount determined by local governments according to various factors, such as the cost to manage the child's institution (Ministry of Education and Research, 2014a).

Basic Education

The Ministry of Education and Research (2014b) defines basic education as minimum compulsory education and indicates that it starts when children turn seven years of age. However, children below age seven may start basic education if their preschool child care institution or the advisory commission determines they are ready. Several choices exist on how students can complete basic education. Students can attend the school that the local government assigns them or receive home schooling if their parents request this option. They can also send their children to a school outside their catchment area if the school has a place.

Before attending primary school, a school readiness report needs to be submitted to the school. This report is usually provided by a preschool child care institution. Although students usually attend school at their area of residence without entry tests, some schools use them. Such schools offer intensive classes and use tests to evaluate children's abilities (Ministry of Education and Research, 2014b).

School breaks except for the summer break typically last one or two weeks with the dates determined by the Minister of Education and Research. The break periods for the 2014–2015 academic year are listed below:

- Fall Break—October 18—October 26, 2014
- Christmas Break—December 20, 2014—January 4, 2015
- Spring Break—March 14—March 22, 2015
- Summer Break—June 4—August 31, 2015

Although many methods are implemented to assess student progress, the usual way involves rating students according to a five-point scale: 5 = very good, 4 = good, 3 = satisfactory, 2 = poor, and 1 = weak. If students satisfy the requirements for basic education, they graduate with a certificate. To achieve this goal, students need to earn school marks at least at the satisfactory level and complete a creative project. In addition, they need to receive at least a satisfactory mark on the Estonian language exam, mathematics exam, and another exam in a subject they select (Ministry of Education and Research, 2014b).

Upper Secondary Education

Upper secondary education follows basic education for students who choose to enroll. It consists of non-compulsory education that lasts for three years. For students to successfully complete this level and earn a certificate, they need to fulfill the following requirements:

- Earn a mark of at least satisfactory or for elective courses satisfactory or pass.
- Earn at least a satisfactory on state examinations in mathematics, a foreign language, and Estonian or Estonian as a second language.

- Earn at least a satisfactory on the school leaving exam.
- Complete a research project or practical assignment (not required for part time students).

Two types of upper secondary education exist: general secondary education and vocational secondary education. The goal of upper secondary education is to prepare students for higher education or vocational institutions. Students may also enroll in upper secondary education part-time if they hold a job but still want to pursue their education. Such students usually attend different schools referred to as "upper secondary schools for adults." Most students in Estonia who enroll at the upper secondary school level attend mainstream schools, and about 1/6 attend secondary schools for adults. Only 16 part-time upper secondary schools for adults operated during the 2013/2014 academic year, but 202 mainstream upper secondary schools functioned the same year (Ministry of Education and Research, 2015).

A significant number of upper secondary students (30%) enroll in vocational education. Although a national curriculum does not exist for vocational education, professional councils develop standards that serve as the foundation for the vocational school curriculum. These standards also measure learning outcomes (Delaney & Kraemer, n.d.).

Curriculum

The national curriculum in Estonia was adopted by the government during the 1997/1998 academic year. This curriculum is intended to fulfill the following functions:

- Defines learning objectives.
- Identifies cross-curricular topics.
- Recommends methods for organizing the learning environment.
- Specifies the areas of assessment involving students' knowledge and defines the requirements for graduation from compulsory school.
- Determines the strategies for preparing the school curriculum.

The national curriculum includes mathematics, science, language and literature, foreign languages, social studies, art, technology, and physical education. It also includes components on communications, self-management, entrepreneurship, and learning-to-learn. The following subjects are compulsory: mathematics, a foreign language, Estonian literature (for Estonian track schools), and Estonian language (for Russian track schools) (Delaney & Kraemer, n.d.).

Although the national curriculum sets certain objectives, each school needs to create its own curriculum within the framework of the national curriculum. Although the school director approves the school-level curriculum, the development of this curriculum involves the board of trustees, the school staff, the student council, and the teacher council. Despite making decisions on curriculum content, some schools have raised concerns regarding not having enough flexibility to develop it (Santiago et al., 2016).

School Autonomy

While concerns have been raised regarding a need for more flexibility, schools in Estonia enjoy a considerable level of autonomy. Schools are responsible for creating a plan of change to improve instruction. This plan is typically designed for the unique circumstances and needs of the local area, parents, students, and school staff (Delaney & Kraemer, n.d.).

Indeed, with regard to the decision-making process, Estonia has one of the most decentralized school systems. A survey indicated that although the OECD average for making decisions at the school level was about 41% in 2010–2011, in Estonia 76% of the decisions were made at the school level. Estonia has also gained a reputation as standing out from other countries with regard to having high levels of autonomy over the allocation of teaching staff (Santiago et al., 2016).

This high level of school autonomy is also reflected in the way schools are held accountable. Whereas in the United States a rather punitive approach based primarily on standardized test results has been used at public schools in the 21st century, in Estonia a better approach is implemented. Inspectors there assess schools on a number of components, including their teaching and learning process, preparation, and leadership. They look for strengths and weaknesses and report if areas needing improvement exist. If a school is not following regulations, they have authority to revoke its license (Delaney & Kraemer, n.d.).

School directors often perform this process; however, sometimes other individuals participate:

> The school director is responsible for regular internal appraisal, but may delegate this authority to lower positions in the school, such as the deputy school director. Other individuals, including the chairs of subject sections and methodology associ-

ations, may also participate in the process, depending on the size and organisational structure of the school. Schools have a high degree of autonomy regarding the way they implement regular teacher appraisal for performance management. School directors are expected to determine the aims, criteria and methods of appraisal, while accounting for the school's specific context, educational programme and priorities. The appraisal generally involves classroom observation. School directors may write an evaluation report regarding the performance of each teacher and store it within the teacher's file. (Santiago et al., 2016, pp. 200–201)

School principals have the power to hire and fire staff. They also have the authority to negotiate job contracts and make budget decisions (OECD, 2016).

Students with Special Needs

An effort is made when practical to place students with special needs in regular classes in Estonia. However, some students are placed in special classes in mainstream schools, and others attend special education schools. Children with special needs are considered those who have conditions requiring significant adjustments to facilitate their learning. To determine if a child has a special need, various methods may be used including a medical exam, a behavioral observation, and a psychological assessment. Various methods, including standardized tests and results in national or international subject Olympiads, are used to identify gifted students (Santiago et al., 2016).

The adjustments students with special needs most often receive include extra help after classes, differentiated instruction, speech therapy sessions, and an individual learning curriculum. The individual curriculum consists of a personalized curriculum specifying the optimal conditions that will promote the child's progress. It can be designed for one, a few, or all subjects (Ministry of Education and Research, 2016).

Mainstream schools normally have a special educational needs coordinator responsible for managing the services students with special needs require. This coordinator makes sure that support specialists and teachers collaborate well and establishes a working relationship with various individuals including support specialists, teachers, and parents (Santiago et al., 2016).

Students who need facilities unavailable in mainstream schools attend special education schools. Most of these schools are state or municipal schools, but a few private ones exist. All such schools receive support from the state even if private. Students at these schools have visual, speech, or hearing impairments, or emotional and behavioral disorders. Others have mobility or intellectual disabilities. Some of these students have an interest in pursuing vocational education; however, this form of education is unavailable at these special schools. Consequently, these students take it at regular vocational schools. In 2013, the percentage of these students was very small (6%) when compared with the total number of vocational education students. Such students are usually combined with other students in regular classes, but sometimes they are placed in a special group if such a group may enhance their learning (Santiago et al., 2016).

Historical Background

In addition to investigating Estonia's curriculum, school structure, and educational policies to see how these components contribute to the country's high scores, exploring the country from a historical perspective offers reasons as well. Some of the events that led the Estonian people to have a desire to learn, for example, happened centuries ago.

Estonia's Previous Education Systems

During the 18th century, Estonia was ruled by Russia. During this time, many adults taught themselves to read and write as a result of the influence of church leaders who encouraged literacy among the Estonian people. Parents passed these skills on to their children, leading a large percentage of the population to be literate (OECD, 2016). By 1881, it was estimated that 94% of the population at age 14 and above could read, and 48% were able to read and write (Põldma & Puur, n.d.).

Estonia was an independent state for a brief time early in the 20th century. When it became independent in 1918, a public education system was set up, and Estonian became the language of instruction. Estonia became part of the Soviet Union in 1940, and its education system was restructured to reflect Soviet ideals. For example, the curriculum emphasized Russian as the language of instruction. Despite Soviet influence, schools had some autonomy with regard to the language of instruction and the development of the curriculum. At the same time, schools with Russian as the language of instruction were created to serve the increasing number of Russian migrants (Põldma & Puur, n.d.).

Reforms in the 1980s and 1990s

Reforms started in the late 1980s and shaped the education system that exists today. At a teachers' meeting in 1987, approximately 1,000 teachers objected to the Soviet method of education. The Soviet curriculum focused on factual knowledge rather than on problem solving. Even before Estonia gained its independence in 1991, schools using Estonian as the language of instruction started to plan lessons according to a new curriculum. The new curriculum supported the new market economy and the end of communist rule. It focused on problem solving, critical thinking, and personal responsibility (OECD, 2016).

Estonia borrowed ideas from Finland to develop its new school system after gaining independence. Estonian school leaders consulted with Finnish education experts to develop the new curriculum. Some of the components believed to contribute to Estonia's current success, including allowing schools to have high levels of autonomy for curriculum and learning outcomes, were borrowed from the Finnish approach to education (OECD, 2016).

More Recent Reforms

More reforms occurred in the 21st century. These reforms were a response to international test scores showing that students in Russian-language schools scored significantly lower than those in Estonian-language schools. The government responded by doing more to promote equal educational opportunities. Additional resources, such as study material, were provided to Russian teachers. In addition, Russian teachers were provided with support to become proficient in the Estonian language so that they can attend professional development sessions at Estonian-language schools (OECD, 2016).

Estonia has also increased its effort to ensure that all students regardless of income level have basic services. Since 2006, for example, all students have been provided with free hot school lunches and learning materials (NCEE, n.d.-a).

Areas Needing Improvement

Several areas pertaining to Estonia's educational system may cause a decline in its impressive ranking in international testing in the near future. Although Estonia's scores on international tests are remarkable, the low salaries teachers earn and the rigid curriculum could lead to a decrease in the quality of the school system.

In addition to being poorly paid despite efforts to raise their salaries, Estonian teachers endure an unusually heavy workload. Although this aspect of the educational system contributes to its efficiency, it could backfire soon, leading to big problems. Further, the Estonian approach to teaching is very traditional in part because parents usually complain when teachers deviate from teaching textbook content. Consequently, businesses may endure problems due to the lack of graduates with workplace skills. Estonia's rigid curriculum will likely lead to difficulties for Estonia unless changes are made:

> The only way to prevent a fall in Estonia's standard of living will be to increase the productivity of Estonia's workers. But that will not happen unless Estonia embraces a curriculum that is much more applied, much less tied to the textbook, much more focused on helping students learn how to set their own goals, frame their own problems, work collaboratively with other students to achieve those goals and address those problems and start acting as if work and learning go together, inextricably, rather than thinking of learning as something that you do before you go to work. That will require a revolution in Estonia. And the parents will have to buy into that revolution or it will not happen. (Tucker, 2015, para. 6)

According to an OECD (2016) report, the most urgent problem involves the teachers. Because teachers have low status, it will be difficult to attract qualified candidates in the future.

Another problem Estonia is dealing with involves the inadequate support for Russian-speaking students. Although reforms were implemented to close the academic gap between Russian-speaking and Estonian-speaking students, the gap still persists. The inequalities between these two groups are reflected in the higher percentage of Russian students who attend vocational rather than general upper secondary schools. The vocational curriculum is regarded as a track for students who lack the skills needed to succeed in the academic track (Tucker, 2015).

One reason a higher percentage of Russian students enroll in vocational secondary schools relates to the language of instruction available at these schools. Whereas Russian has been discontinued as a language of instruction in general upper secondary education, in vocational school it is still available. In addition, basic schools with Russian as the language of instruction have been reported to teach Estonian ineffectively, making it less likely for many Russian students to continue their education in a school where Russian is not the language of instruction (Santiago et al., 2016).

The Estonian educational system has also been criticized for not doing more to enhance the education of students with special needs. The problem involves the little progress that has been made to combine children with special needs with other students in regular schools. Many parents believe their children will not get enough attention at mainstream schools, so they keep their children in special schools. Teachers at mainstream schools often have trouble when students with special needs attend their classes, most likely because they lack the preparation to teach these students (Santiago et al., 2016).

Conclusion

Like many other top-performing nations in education, Estonia is ranked highly as a result of some exemplary practices that allow its students to perform well academically. The most important of these involves the educational opportunities economically disadvantaged students have. Unlike the United States, Estonia has a relatively high percentage of low-income students who perform well on the PISA (OECD, 2013).

In addition to providing sufficient educational opportunities for low-income students, some of the lessons the United States can learn from Estonia involve the efficiency of its education system and the success Estonia achieved after borrowing ideas from abroad. Critics of using the education methods that top-performing nations apply argue that the education system is only one component of many that explain the academic achievement of students. However, Estonia and some of the other countries covered in this book benefited from this approach. With regard to efficiency, expenditure on education per student in Estonia is lower than in most OECD countries (Tucker, n.d.). For example, in contrast to Estonia, the United States spends much more per student than other OECD countries (Ryan, 2013).

Unfortunately, Estonia's efficient system comes at a price. Whereas other top-performing systems also spend less than the United States, they do so and still pay their teachers adequately. This practice does not occur in Estonia because teachers there are poorly paid. As a result of the low pay and the exhausting workload, Estonia is currently having problems recruiting teachers. In addition, the academic curriculum does little to develop the skills students need to thrive in the work environment. To make matters worse, Estonia's population is decreasing as the number of retirees is growing. These factors mean that Estonia needs to increase the productivity of its workers to support the increasing number of retirees through an applied curriculum instead of the traditional approach schools currently use. If schools continue to function with the same curriculum and low teacher salaries, the country could very well experience a decline not only in test scores but also in the standard of living (Tucker, n.d.).

Estonia has a good chance of achieving high scores in the near future because when it previously reformed, it borrowed ideas from its northern neighbor, Finland. If it continues to borrow policies similar to Finland's and starts to offer teachers the salaries they deserve in addition to improving its curriculum, Estonia may be able to counteract the concerns involving its educational system. Only time will tell whether Estonia will make the needed reforms to avoid a downfall.

References

Butrymowicz, S. (2016, June 23). Is Estonia the new Finland? *The Atlantic*. Retrieved from https://www.theatlantic.com/education/archive/2016/06/is-estonia-the-new-finland/488351/

Delaney, A., & Kraemer, J. (n.d.). Estonia: A shining light in Eastern Europe. *National Center on Education and the Economy*. Retrieved from http://ncee.org/2014/05/global-perspectives-estonia-a-shining-light-in-eastern-europe/

EP-Nuffic. (2015). *Education system Estonia*. Retrieved from https://www.nuffic.nl/en/publications/find-a-publication/education-system-estonia.pdf

Jackson, A., & Kiersz, A. (2016). The latest ranking of top countries in math, reading, and science is out—and the US didn't crack the top 10. *Business Insider*. Retrieved from http://www.businessinsider.com/pisa-worldwide-ranking-of-math-science-reading-skills-2016-12

Ministry of Education and Research. (2014a). *Pre-school education*. Retrieved from https://www.hm.ee/en/activities/pre-school-basic-and-secondary-education/pre-school-education

Ministry of Education and Research. (2014b). *Basic education*. Retrieved from https://www.hm.ee/en/activities/pre-school-basic-and-secondary-education/basic-education

Ministry of Education and Research. (2015). *Secondary education*. Retrieved from https://www.hm.ee/en/activities/pre-school-basic-and-secondary-education/secondary-education

Ministry of Education and Research. (2016). *Special educational needs*. Retrieved from https://www.hm.ee/en/activities/pre-school-basic-and-secondary-education/special-educational-needs

National Center on Education and the Economy. (n.d.-a). *Estonia: Equity*. Retrieved from http://ncee.org/what-we-do/center-on-international-education-benchmarking/top-performing-countries/estonia-overview/estonia-equity/

National Center on Education and the Economy. (n.d.-b). *Estonia: Teacher and principal quality*. Retrieved from http://ncee.org/what-we-do/center-on-international-education-benchmarking/top-performing-countries/estonia-overview/estonia-teacher-and-principal-quality/

Organization for Economic Cooperation and Development. (2013). *PISA 2012 results: What makes schools successful? Resources, policies and practices* (Vol. IV). Paris: Organization of Economic Cooperation and Development.

Organization for Economic Cooperation and Development. (2016). *PISA 2015 high performers: Estonia*. Retrieved from https://www.oecd.org/pisa/PISA-2015-estonia.pdf

Põldma, A., & Puur, A. (n.d.). Educational policies: Estonia (2014). *Population Europe Resource Finder & Archive*. Retrieved from http://www.perfar.eu/policy/education/estonia

Ryan, J. (2013, December 3). American schools vs. the world: Expensive, unequal, bad at math. *The Atlantic*. Retrieved from https://www.theatlantic.com/education/archive/2013/12/american-schools-vs-the-world-expensive-unequal-bad-at-math/281983/

Santiago, P., Levitas, A., Radó, P., & Shewbridge, C. (2016). *OECD reviews of school resources: Estonia 2016*. Paris: Organization of Economic Co-operation and Development.

Tucker, M. (n.d.). Tucker's lens: Estonia: Unsung heroine of the Baltic, but... *National Center on Education and the Economy*. Retrieved from http://ncee.org/2015/03/tuckers-lens-estonia-unsung-heroine-of-the-baltic-but/

Tucker, M. (2015, April 9). Estonia's education system: Full of promise, facing challenges. *Education Week*. Retrieved from http://blogs.edweek.org/edweek/top_performers/2015/04/promise_and_challenge_in_estonia.html

· 9 ·

FROM EXCELLENCE TO MEDIOCRITY

The Decline of the Education System in the United States

Ever since the first international assessment was offered in the 1960s, the United States generally has experienced less than optimal results on international tests. On some occasions, American students performed well, as I pointed out in Chapter 1, but they have never scored at the very top. Despite its overall unimpressive results, the United States was regarded as the undisputed world leader in education in the 1970s (Darling-Hammond, 2014). How could have the United States been the undisputed leader in education if its students never scored at the very top? The answer has to do with other statistics that show it held the lead in other components involving education.

This chapter will explore the impressive accomplishments the United States has achieved in education and the factors leading to its decline, but first I will discuss its results on the 2015 PISA and the factors that contribute to these outcomes. On this test, American students continued to perform at a less than optimal level, achieving about average scores in reading and science and below average scores in math (OECD, 2016).

As in previous years, inequalities among different groups continue to be a problem in the United States. Most of the countries covered in this book have a much better record with regard to the performance of their low-income students. Although the United States improved dramatically in this area in science on the 2015 PISA, it did not match many top-performing countries with respect to the percentages of low-income students who achieve high scores. Socioeconomic status explained 11% of the difference in American students' science scores in 2015. This percentage is a little better than the average percentage for the developed world and a big improvement over the United States' percentage in 2006 when its socioeconomic status explained 17% of this difference. Although the United States made more progress on this metric in 2015 than any other country, it still did not match the leading countries in this area (Ripley, 2016).

Inequalities in Education

The evidence that other countries provide more opportunities for low-income students to excel includes school principals' perceptions of the resources available for these students and the fewer hours of instruction low-income students receive. Principals working in socioeconomically disadvantaged schools in Finland, Estonia, Korea, Germany, and Slovenia tend to say their schools have as many, if not more, resources than those in wealthier areas (OECD, 2013a). However, their counterparts in the United States are more inclined to say their schools lack the human resources that schools in wealthier districts have. As for instruction hours, privileged students in the United States average 50 minutes more of science instruction per week in school than low-income students (OECD, 2016).

The severe inequalities in education that persist in the United States can be explained from a historical perspective. From the earliest days of the United States' history, people of non-European descent were treated with severe forms of discrimination that still manifests itself today in various ways. Native Americans, for example, were forced to leave the areas they inhabited to live on reservations, a pattern of isolation and inequity that has persisted until today (Gollnick & Chinn, 2013).

Native Americans also endured inequalities in education. They were prevented from practicing aspects of their culture when they had to assimilate in the late 1800s at boarding schools. Other non-European groups were mistreated. For example, Chinese children were regularly denied admission to schools in the 1800s because of their ancestry. Even after the *Tape vs. Hurley* case (1885), which granted them the right to attend public schools, they were forced to attend segregated schools. Latino students also endured inequalities at the turn of the 20th century when they were denied equal educational opportunities (Noltemeyer, Mujic, & McLoughlin, 2012).

Like all other racial minority groups, Africans endured horrific inequalities in society and schools. In the South, state laws made it illegal to teach slaves to read and write during the 1800s. Although a few efforts were made to educate people of African descent, the majority of whites continued to suppress their education. Although Jim Crow laws allowing African people to be educated were passed in the late 1800s, they had to attend racially segregated schools that were usually inferior in quality. Although the *Brown vs. Board of Education* case overturned the Jim Crow laws in 1954, progress was slow with violent resistance especially in the South, sometimes requiring military force to protect African American students. Despite the passing of the Federal Civil Rights Act of 1964, which prohibited discrimination against various groups, de facto segregation continued in the 1970s and 1980s. Although by the mid-1980s integration had increased considerably, resurgence in racial segregation occurred later, persisting until today and leading to severe inequalities in the 21st century. Some of its causes included increased school choice, changes in residential patterns, and court decisions that counteracted previous improvements (Noltemeyer et al., 2012).

Court Decisions

Despite these severe inequalities, racial minority groups have made significant improvements in education. For example, universities are experiencing an increase in African American student enrollment. However, a significant achievement gap between racial minority and white students persists. In addition, the resurgence of racial segregation has not slowed down in K–12 schools (Mujic, 2015).

Racial segregation has increased to a great extent as a result of court decisions releasing schools from earlier mandates requiring districts to desegregate. In Tuscaloosa, for example, city schools no longer had to adhere to the desegregation mandate that was previously in place in 2000 because a federal judge overturned it. District representatives argued that because schools integrated successfully, the desegregation mandate was no longer needed. The Tuscaloosa district was one of the most successful districts in the South to integrate and was the home of Central High School. This school became known for its academic success a few years after a federal judge ordered the integration of two segregated schools in 1979. Today, this school no longer exists, and the desegregated schools are gone. Although the city's schools may not be as segregated as they were in 1954, a dramatic decline in the improvements made in previous years is noticeable (Hannah-Jones, 2014).

Furthermore, what happened in Tuscaloosa is not endemic to Alabama:

> Certainly what happened in Tuscaloosa was no accident. Nor was it isolated. Schools in the South, once the most segregated in the country, had by the 1970s become the most integrated, typically as a result of federal court orders. But since 2000, judges have released hundreds of school districts, from Mississippi to Virginia, from court-enforced integration, and many of these districts have followed the same path as Tuscaloosa's—back toward segregation. Black children across the South now attend majority-black schools at levels not seen in four decades. Nationally, the achievement gap between black and white students, which greatly narrowed during the era in which schools grew more integrated, widened as they became less so. (Hannah-Jones, 2014, para. 10)

Some schools are now so segregated that researchers refer to them as apartheid schools because they have a white population that is 1% or less. Most of these schools are in the Midwest and Northeast, but over 10% of blacks attend such schools in the South. Over 50% of black students in districts where desegregation mandates were repealed between 1990 and 2011 were estimated to attend such schools in 2014, and this percentage will grow if desegregation mandates continue to be overturned (Hannah-Jones, 2014).

When poor black and Latino students are segregated from everyone else and sent to inferior schools like in Tuscaloosa and other regions of the United States, fewer opportunities exist to close the achievement gap. As Chapter 1 mentioned, the inequalities students in poor districts endure prevent them from making academic gains that may narrow the achievement gap. This gap is large not only at the K–12 level but at the higher education level as well.

Despite these inequalities, Hispanic and black dropout rates recently reached record lows, according to the Pew Research Center. The Hispanic dropout rate dropped dramatically from 32% in 2000 to 12% in 2014, helping to reduce the national dropout rate to a new low. In addition, the number of Hispanics enrolled in colleges increased by 13% from 1993 to 2014. However, these achievements do not show important differences between these groups and whites that reveal a large gap in academic achievement. As of 2014, for example, among Hispanics in the 25 to 29 age range, only 15% of them held a bachelor's degree or higher, compared with 41% of whites in the same age range. In addition, almost half of Hispanics attend community colleges or two-year schools, compared with 30% of whites (Krogstad, 2016).

Large achievement gaps also persist at the high school level. Fifty years after the Coleman Report suggested that about 87% of white 12th graders outperformed the average black 12th grader in both math and reading, the gap is still large. In 2015, it was estimated that in math the average black 12th grader was at the 19th percentile of the white distribution, and in reading at the 22nd percentile. Eric Hanushek (2015) called the failure to further narrow the achievement gap between white and black students a national embarrassment:

> After nearly a half century of supposed progress in race relations within the United States, the modest improvements in achievement gaps since 1965 can only be called a national embarrassment. Put differently, if we continue to close gaps at the same rate in the future, it will be roughly two and a half centuries before the black-white math gap closes and over one and a half centuries until the reading gap closes. If "Equality of Educational Opportunity" was expected to mobilize the resources of the nation's schools in pursuit of racial equity, it undoubtedly failed to achieve its objective. Nor did it increase the overall level of performance of high school students on the eve of their graduation, despite the vast increase in resources that would be committed to education over the ensuing five decades[.] (pp. 21–22)

Charter Schools

The expansion of charter schools in the 21st century has contributed to the increasing segregation in the American school system. Charter schools segregate students not only by race and socioeconomic status but also by language and disability (Economic Policy Institute, 2016). This problem is more serious today because since 2000 the ratio of charter to public schools has increased considerably (Rotberg, 2014).

Charter schools promote inequality and segregation as a result of the methods they use to admit certain groups of students as they prevent others from enrolling. Because these schools suffered the same sanctions as public schools for failing to perform well under NCLB, many of them created ways to limit students from low-income families and any others who may not perform well academically. For example, after taking over a public school in Minneapolis, a charter school requested that forty autistic students enroll at another school (Ravitch, 2013).

One of the ways charter schools keep students not likely to perform well academically from enrolling includes offering a limited number of services or programs that appeal only to families without children with special needs. Other tactics include creating burdensome parental involvement requirements that dysfunctional families cannot meet and expelling students who cannot adhere to academic or behavioral requirements. Another method involves opening schools at locations that create transportation problems for low-income students (Rotberg, 2014).

The ways that charter schools operate not only promote segregation but also harm the public school system. In her book on the privatization movement, Diane Ravitch (2013) provided a few examples of how charter schools damage the public school system. One of her examples involves a district in Inglewood, California. This district endured limited resources but also produced students with high test scores. Bennett-Kew Elementary School, one of the district's schools, produced results so impressive that it was recognized as one of the best schools in the country. Unfortunately, a large number of the district's students enrolled in charter schools from 2003 to 2011, forcing it to lay off teachers and to increase its class sizes. Although the state eventually took control of this district and allocated an emergency loan to avoid bankruptcy, hoping students would return, this effort failed.

A similar case involving children who left a public school district to attend a charter school occurred at the Chester Upland School District. This district lost about half of its students, causing it to be nearly bankrupt. Other districts in Pennsylvania were having the same trouble when this event happened. As this process continues, towns become in danger of losing their public education system to charter schools with operators who can make profits by increasing classes as they reduce teachers, salaries, and programs (Ravitch, 2013).

For charter schools to promote integration, more provisions that encourage diversity are needed. Although a small number of charter schools are designed to promote diversity, most of them use methods that lead to segregation (Rotberg, 2014). This outcome is regrettable because charter schools were designed to support the neediest students and to encourage innovative practices. Instead, many of them find ways to keep low-income students from enrolling. In addition, they often operate according to antiquated methods of teaching based on strict discipline and rigid routines similar to the style of teaching used in the United States in the early 1900s (Ravitch, 2013).

A Leading Country in Education in Previous Years

The increasing inequalities in education caused by practices that promote segregation prevents the United States from achieving high scores on international tests. In previous years, when it did not allow the severe inequalities that exist today and when it accomplished educational goals other countries had not achieved, the United States produced impressive outcomes. These outcomes led some researchers to consider it the world leader in education even though American students never performed especially well on international tests. What were these outcomes? These results included a highly educated work force, record setting high school graduation rates, and a large quantity of Nobel Prize winners.

Yong Zhao (2012) pointed out that international tests do not measure certain crucial components of education, such as creativity. Creativity is a critical aspect of teaching because it prepares students to come up with discoveries that may alleviate or solve problems. This quality allows Nobel Prize winners to come up with new and more efficient ways to deal with problems or invent methods that benefit society. Although the United States has never performed particularly well on international tests, it has produced over 300 Nobel Prize winners, more than any other country in the world. Although Japan usually outscores the United States by a wide margin, it has produced less than 30 Nobel Prize winners, and China is not even on the list of the top 10 countries with the most Nobel Prize winners (Smith, 2016).

Could it be that in the area of creativity and discovery, the United States is better than the leading countries in international testing? China is much more populated than the United States, so it seems evident that their rigid educational system has for many years not prepared their students to be creative. The United States has less than three times the population of Japan (Central Intelligence Agency, n.d.) but has produced well over three times the number of Novel Prize winners than Japan. Such statistics imply that the United States is indeed more advanced than the East Asian nations in the kind of education that promotes creativity because it has produced more Nobel Prize winners per capita than these countries. However, some countries such as Germany, Israel, the United Kingdom, and Sweden have produced more Nobel Prize winners per capita than the United States. The reason the United States surpassed these countries in education when it was the world leader in education involves other remarkable accomplishments these nations did not achieve.

At one point in history, for example, the United states had a system that produced not only the best high school graduation rates in the world but also other accomplishments that rivaled the world's leading education systems. Regarding high school graduation rates, the United States led the world in this category in the late 1960s. Further, it was tied for first place in the ratio of young adults with a college degree in 1995. Regrettably, these accomplishments declined by the 21st century. By 2006, the United States had dropped to 14th place in the ratio of young adults with a college degree, a rank that put it below the OECD average for the first time. By 2006, it had also lost the lead in high school graduation rates by a considerable margin, slipping to 18th out of 24 industrialized nations (Jerald, 2008). In addition to its lackluster PISA scores in the 21st century, the United States' school system is currently not ranked highly at the international level because many nations have better high school graduation rates. A record high 83% of students in the United States' earned a high school diploma in the 2014–2015 school year (Brown & Matos, 2016). However, the OECD reported in 2014 that the United States had some of the lowest graduation rates among the industrialized nations and that only Greece, Mexico, Luxembourg, and Austria had lower rates (Mason, 2015).

Before its graduation rates declined, the United States made other notable progress in education that helped it gain recognition as a world leader in education. For example, it was the first country to create universal secondary education. It also increased enrollment in higher education after World War II by implementing the G.I. Bill, which helped the United States to have the most educated workforce in the world (Stewart, 2012). Additionally, the United States is where some of the most influential figures in education, including John Dewey, were educated. Some of the countries now experiencing success in international testing have implemented practices based on theories of teaching that originated in the United States. For example, Finland created its new education system based on the democratic idea that all students are capable of learning, an idea that John Dewey promoted generations earlier (Sahlberg, 2012).

Teacher Pay

One of the reasons the United States lost its status as a world leader in education involves the low salaries teachers currently earn. Low salaries do not attract the qualified people needed for students to learn optimally. An OECD

(2013b) report, for example, mentioned that in high-income countries that perform highly in math, teachers usually earn a good salary.

To highlight the inadequate pay American teachers earn, Dick Startz (2016) investigated the difference in earnings between teachers in the United States and those in Finland, a country that pays its teachers a modest salary. He concluded that to raise American teachers' salaries to a level equivalent to what teachers in Finland earn, schools would need to pay primary teachers 10% more, lower secondary teachers 18% more, and upper secondary teachers 28% more.

In 2012, the United States paid its lower secondary teachers a salary that was not only lower than the salaries of lower secondary teachers in Estonia, a country known for not paying its teachers well, but also lower than the OECD average (OECD, 2014a). Figure 9.1 shows an OECD chart comparing lower secondary teachers' salaries relative to earnings for tertiary-educated workers aged 25–64.

Figure 9.1: Teachers' salaries relative to earnings for tertiary-educated workers aged 25–64 (2012)

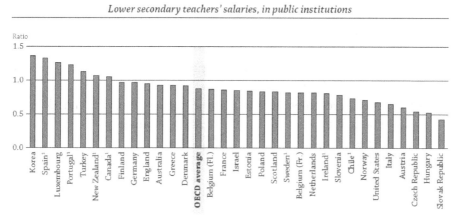

Lower secondary teachers' salaries, in public institutions

Source: OECD (2014b, Chart D.3.1).

People may feel that great teachers do not pursue their careers for the money but for the love of teaching. Although this perception is accurate, many qualified people in the United States who may love teaching at the K–12 level probably choose a different profession simply to provide what is needed for their families to thrive (Startz, 2016).

Respect for Teachers

In addition to low pay, some students in the United States will likely not choose to pursue a career in teaching because of the low prestige associated with it. Although data on factors involving the way parents and administrators treat teachers is scarce, it is likely that in other industrialized countries, respect for teachers is greater than in the United States (Startz, 2016).

In Finland, for example, teachers receive the same respect as doctors and lawyers. The respect for the teaching profession in Finland increased after a decision reformers made in 1979 that would require teachers to have a master's degree. After this reform, teacher shortage problems became nonexistent:

> The second critical decision came in 1979, when reformers required that every teacher earn a fifth-year master's degree in theory and practice at one of eight state universities—at state expense. From then on, teachers were effectively granted equal status with doctors and lawyers. Applicants began flooding teaching programs, not because the salaries were so high but because autonomy and respect made the job attractive. (Hancock, 2011, para. 30)

Unfortunately, teachers in the United States sometimes enter the profession with minimal requirements. Oklahoma is a state where this problem has worsened. This state recently experienced a record number of students taught by a teacher with an emergency certificate, a certificate permitting people without a teaching degree to teach in public schools. To receive this certificate, adults without a degree in teaching need to pass a criminal background check and a test in the subject they want to teach. A teacher shortage task force based in Oklahoma suggested new ideas it hopes will alleviate the problem. It is believed that teacher pay in Oklahoma worsens the problem considerably because teacher salaries there are some of the lowest in the United States (Felder, 2016).

The Teacher Shortage Problem

The low pay and lack of prestige associated with the teaching profession lead to teacher shortage problems not only in Oklahoma but also in many other states. In 2016, for example, California was reported to have teacher shortages throughout the state in almost every subject. The negativity associated with the teaching profession has recently contributed to a large drop in enrollment in teacher preparation programs. Other factors that contribute to the teacher shortage problem include high teacher turnover rates and teacher retirements. Like in Oklahoma, this problem leads other states to make it easier for candidates to enter the teaching profession. Such a practice, rather than solving the problem, contributes strongly to high teacher turnover rates because teachers with little preparation not only struggle in helping students to learn but also leave the profession faster. In addition, American taxpayers pay for this problem because over 2 billion dollars is spent annually on replacing teachers (Polakow-Suransky, Thomases, & Demoss, 2016).

For the United States to be more competitive with top-performing nations, it needs to ensure that highly qualified teachers are available for all students. This goal will not materialize if qualified teachers who leave the profession are replaced with teachers with minimal qualifications. Unfortunately, this trend is the one that America currently experiences.

As mentioned previously, in comparison with the top-performing nations, the United States has an attrition rate considerably higher, in some cases over twice as high. Solving this problem requires an awareness of reasons other than teacher pay and prestige that may lead teachers to leave the profession. One of these other reasons involves unsupportive administrators. In fact, teachers who perceive their administrators as unsupportive are more than twice as likely to leave the profession. Other reasons relate to concerns about time for planning and collegial relationships (Sutcher, Darling-Hammond, & Carver-Thomas, 2016). Some strategies for solving this problem are discussed in Chapter 10.

What will alleviate or solve this problem? The solution does not involve lowering standards as some states are currently doing. Although proceeding this way may work temporarily, in the long run, it will backfire in several ways. First, underprepared teachers are much more likely to leave the profession, thereby continuing the high turnover problem and costing taxpayers millions of dollars to replace them. Second, the achievement gap will continue to exist because schools in low-income districts with high numbers of minority students get much higher percentages of teachers with minimal qualifications than other schools (Sutcher et al., 2016).

Structure of the School System

In order for Americans to enact reforms to improve the United States' education system, an understanding of its school structure is crucial. The education system in America is decentralized; each state has power over individual schools as well as higher education institutions. In contrast to countries with centralized education systems that perform the fiscal, administrative, and political components, state and territorial governments in the United States perform these functions. Some of the duties they perform include providing funding for all levels of public schools, determining curriculum policies, and licensing teachers. The role of the federal government is limited and includes providing leadership, enforcing civil rights laws involving education, and providing national and international educational statistics. At the local level, school boards govern the districts. These boards consist of elected citizens who oversee operations, budgets, and staff (U.S. Department of Education, 2008).

In addition to traditional public schools, various types of other schools exist, including private schools, charter schools, and magnet schools. Private schools appoint their own boards of trustees and create their own admissions policies and curriculum. In 2013, enrollment at these schools had dropped from 12% to 10%. This drop is expected to continue despite programs some states have enacted that provide publicly funded vouchers to parents who send their children to these schools. One of the reasons for the decrease in private schools relates to the increase in charter schools, which allow parents more options to send their children to different types of schools without having to pay tuition. Many private schools are affiliated with a specific religion, and others, although not attached to a denomination, have a religious orientation (Jennings, 2013).

Although charter schools are public schools, they use a special curriculum or instructional practices. Students from any parts of a given district can apply to a charter school, and these schools do not have to adhere to school district regulations. Such schools were organized in the early 1990s and receive public funding. They operate through an agreement that defines the school's mission (U.S. Department of Education, 2008).

Magnet schools are part of the public school system; however, unlike charter schools, teachers there need to adhere to district rules. Whereas private companies operate charter schools, the public school system has complete control of magnet schools. The goal of these schools is to increase diversity. These schools have their own educational theme, and they can accept students from any area in a given district. Critics of these schools contend that they cause problems similar to those that charter schools create, arguing that they have the potential to attract the most motivated students, thereby increasing segregation. On the other hand, proponents say that magnet schools promote academic achievement because they reflect students' interests, encouraging pupils to stay in school and graduate (Rich, 2014).

The Common Core Curriculum

The idea of creating a national set of standards in the United States to ensure all students are taught the same content regardless of where they live started in the 21st century. In the 1990s, each state had its own standards indicating the knowledge and skills students needed to acquire. However, because each state could create its own definition of proficiency, concerns developed as a result of the lack of standardization, leading to the development of the Common Core State Standards in 2009 (Common Core State Standards Initiative, n.d.). These national standards were also created because state leaders felt that more rigorous standards were needed, arguing that high college-remediation rates were a sign that high schools were not preparing students adequately. In addition, many employers expressed disappointment with the literacy and math skill levels of young job applicants (Gewertz, 2015).

The Common Core State Standards consist of descriptions of the skills students need to be taught before they graduate from high school. They do not involve guidelines on what students should do on a daily basis, but include an outline of learning expectations that focus on English/language arts and math. From these guidelines, teachers and district leaders are expected to draft their own curriculums (Gewertz, 2015).

Three components were used to create the Common Core State Standards: feedback from the public, the expertise of teachers and leading thinkers, and exemplary state standards already in existence. Almost 10,000 comments from parents, teachers, and school administrators were received during two public comment periods to formulate the standards. Teachers played a crucial role in the development of the standards. They worked in teams to supply their input on drafts of the standards. They also provided feedback during both public comment sessions (Common Core State Standards Initiative, n.d.).

Although many states have adopted the standards, considerable controversy emerged when they were implemented. A few states reversed their adoptions, and about half of the states decided not to use tests to measure mastery of the standards even though they initially approved of proceeding this way. Most of the backlash is politically motivated. Conservatives believe that the federal government's involvement interferes with states' rights, and liberal activists believe that Common Core limits the way teachers can tailor instruction according to a given communities' needs. Although opponents of the standards argue that the federal government by law cannot determine what is taught in schools, advocates claim that federal officials only encouraged the standards to be implemented. They argue that laws were not violated because these officials did not participate in writing the standards (Gewertz, 2015).

In 2014, the opposition to the standards increased as new groups joined the fight against the use of tests designed to assess students on their mastery of the standards. Several factors triggered opposition to the tests. First, the perception that the federal government had dictated what teachers should teach increased because only two federally funded tests were intended to assess all of America's students rather than state-designed tests. Second, parents and teachers argued that the new tests were more time consuming than most state tests. Third, concerns developed over the role of big corporations. Fear grew over the way companies like Pearson could gain too much influence on educational policy because Pearson had played a role in developing the tests. These factors led thousands of students to boycott the first test designed by the organizations the federal government had funded to create these tests (Gewertz, 2015).

The Every Student Succeeds Act

Chapter 1 pointed out the problems the No Child Left Behind Act of 2001 created. In response to some of these problems, the Every Student Succeeds Act (ESSA) was signed into law on December 10, 2015. This new law was designed to evaluate schools and teachers using a broader range of factors rather than those NCLB required. Although states can pick their own accountability goals, they are expected to narrow gaps in achievement and graduation rates involving the groups furthest behind. In addition to tests, states can use student engagement, postsecondary readiness, or other factors they feel are appropriate as forms of accountability (Klein, 2016).

Because NCLB increased testing and penalized underperforming teachers and schools, contributing to the closing of schools and the firing of teachers, critics perceived it as punitive. When ESSA was passed, politicians including President Obama celebrated, with Mr. Obama calling the legislation a "Christmas miracle." Although ESSA will remain, it will not be applied according to the regulations Mr. Obama wanted to use. Some lawmakers felt these regulations were inappropriate and mentioned they would resist ESSA's goal of decreasing the significance of testing and providing more local control of education (Goldstein, 2017). Only time will tell the extent to which this new legislation will improve or hinder the education system in America.

Conclusion

The United States' public education system has declined considerably since the time scholars considered it the world's leading country in education. Various factors led to this decline, including an increase in inequalities and high teacher turnover rates caused by the low status and low pay associated with the teaching profession.

The inadequate state of the public school system does not have to be a chronic condition. Some of the countries covered in the previous chapters, including Finland and Singapore, transformed their inadequate systems into outstanding systems in a relatively short period of time. The next chapter will offer ideas on how the United States can make similar reforms to regain the lead in education it once held.

References

Brown, E., & Matos, A. (2016, October 17). Nation's high school graduation rate reaches new record high. *The Washington Post*. Retrieved from https://www.washingtonpost.com/news/education/wp/2016/10/17/nations-high-school-graduation-rate-reaches-new-record-high/?utm_term=.8944dd98d634

Central Intelligence Agency. (n.d.). *The world factbook*. Retrieved from https://www.cia.gov/library/publications/the-world-factbook/rankorder/2119rank.html

Common Core State Standards Initiative. (n.d.). *Development process*. Retrieved from http://www.corestandards.org/about-the-standards/development-process/

Darling-Hammond, L. (2014). What can PISA tell us about U.S. education policy? *New England Journal of Public Policy, 26*(1), 1–14.

Economic Policy Institute. (2016). *New study of 11 cities finds the growth of charter schools has increased inequality in education*. Retrieved from http://www.epi.org/press/new-study-of-11-cities-finds-the-growth-of-charter-schools-has-increased-inequality-in-education/

Felder, B. (2016, December 25). Oklahoma sets record for emergency teaching certificates. *The Oklahoman*. Retrieved from http://newsok.com/article/5531924

Gewertz, C. (2015, September 28). The common core explained. *Education Week*. Retrieved from http://www.edweek.org/ew/issues/common-core-state-standards/?cmp=cpc-goog-ew-common+core&ccid=common+core&ccag=common+core&cckw=%2Bcommon%20%2Bcore%20%2Beducation&cccv=content+ad&gclid=COfruby2_NQCFVeewAodZTUOSw#definition

Goldstein, D. (2017, March 9). Obama education rules are swept aside by Congress. *The New York Times*. Retrieved from https://www.nytimes.com/2017/03/09/us/every-student-succeeds-act-essa-congress.html

Gollnick, D. G., & Chinn, P. C. (2013). *Multicultural education in a pluralistic society.* New York, NY: Pearson.

Hancock, L. (2011, September). Why are Finland's schools successful? *Smithsonian Magazine.* Retrieved from http://www.smithsonianmag.com/innovation/why-are-finlands-schools-successful-49859555/

Hannah-Jones, N. (2014, May). Segregation now… *The Atlantic.* Retrieved from https://www.theatlantic.com/magazine/archive/2014/05/segregation-now/359813/

Hanushek, E. A. (2015). What matters for student achievement: Updating Coleman on the influence of families and schools. *Education Next, 16*(2), 18–26.

Jennings, J. (2013, March 28). Proportion of U.S. students in private schools is 10 percent and declining. *The Huffington Post.* Retrieved from http://www.huffingtonpost.com/jack-jennings/proportion-of-us-students_b_2950948.html

Jerald, C. (2008). *Benchmarking for success: Ensuring U.S. students receive a world-class education.* Washington, DC: National Governors Association, Council of Chief State School Officers, and Achieve, Inc.

Klein, A. (2016, March 31). The Every Student Succeeds Act: An ESSA overview. *Education Week.* Retrieved from http://www.edweek.org/ew/issues/every-student-succeeds-act/index.html

Krogstad, J. M. (2016, July 28). 5 facts about Latinos and education. *Pew Research Center.* Retrieved from http://www.pewresearch.org/fact-tank/2016/07/28/5-facts-about-latinos-and-education/

Mason, K. C. (2015, February 12). High school graduation rates rise but U.S. still lags other developed countries. *PBS.* Retrieved from http://www.pbs.org/newshour/rundown/high-school-graduation-rates-tick-u-s-still-lags-developed-countries/

Mujic, J. A. (2015, October 29). Education reform and the failure to fix inequality in America. *The Atlantic.* Retrieved from https://www.theatlantic.com/education/archive/2015/10/education-solving-inequality/412729/

Noltemeyer, A. L., Mujic, J., & McLoughlin, C. S. (2012). The history of inequality in education. In A. L. Noltemeyer & C.S. McLoughlin (Eds.), *Disproportionality in Education and Special Education* (pp. 3–22). Springfield, IL: Charles C. Thomas Publisher.

Organization for Economic Co-operation and Development. (2013a). *PISA 2012 results: What makes schools successful? Resources, policies and practices (Volume IV).* Paris: Organization of Economic Cooperation and Development.

Organization for Economic Co-operation and Development. (2013b). *Strong performers and successful reformers in education: Lessons from PISA 2012 for the United States.* Paris: Organization of Economic Cooperation and Development.

Organization for Economic Co-operation and Development. (2014a). *Indicator D3: How much are teachers paid?* Retrieved from https://www.oecd.org/edu/EAG2014-Indicator%20D3%20(eng).pdf

Organization for Economic Co-operation and Development. (2014b). *Education at a glance 2014: OECD indicators, OECD publishing.* Paris: Organization of Economic Cooperation and Development.

Organization for Economic Co-operation and Development. (2016). *Country note: Key findings from PISA 2015 for the United States*. Paris: Organization of Economic Cooperation and Development.

Polakow-Suransky, S., Thomases, J., & Demoss, K. (2016, July 8). Train teachers like doctors. *The New York Times*. Retrieved from https://www.nytimes.com/2016/07/08/opinion/train-teachers-like-doctors.html

Ravitch, D. (2013). *Reign of error: The hoax of the privatization movement and the danger to America's public schools*. New York, NY: Knopf.

Rich, M. (2014, February 16). Magnet schools find a renewed embrace in cities. *The New York Times*. Retrieved from https://www.nytimes.com/2014/02/17/us/magnet-schools-find-a-renewed-embrace-in-cities.html

Ripley, A. (2016, December 6). What America can learn from smart schools in other countries. *The New York Times*. Retrieved from https://www.nytimes.com/2016/12/06/upshot/what-america-can-learn-about-smart-schools-in-other-countries.html

Rotberg, I. C. (2014). Charter schools and the risk of increased segregation. *Phi Delta Kappan*, 95(5), 26–30.

Sahlberg, P. (2012). A model lesson: Finland shows us what equal opportunity looks like. *American Educator*, 36(1), 20–27.

Smith, O. (2016, December 9). The tiny countries that have produced the most Nobel prize winners per capita. *The Telegraph*. Retrieved from http://www.telegraph.co.uk/travel/maps-and-graphics/countries-nobel-prize-winners-per-capita/

Startz, D. (2016, June 20). Teacher pay around the world. *The Brookings Institution*. Retrieved from https://www.brookings.edu/blog/brown-center-chalkboard/2016/06/20/teacher-pay-around-the-world/

Stewart, V. (2012). *A world-class education: Learning from international models of excellence and innovation*. Alexandria, VA: ASCD.

Sutcher, L., Darling-Hammond, L., & Carver-Thomas, D. (2016). *A coming crisis in teaching? Teacher supply, demand, and shortages in the U.S.* Palo Alto, CA: Learning Policy Institute.

U.S. Department of Education. (2008). *Organization of U.S. education: State role I—Primary and secondary education*. Retrieved from https://www2.ed.gov/about/offices/list/ous/international/usnei/us/edlite-org-us.html

Zhao, Y. (2012, July 17). Doublethink: The creativity-testing conflict. *Education Week*. Retrieved from http://www.edweek.org/ew/articles/2012/07/18/36zhao_ep.h31.html

· 1 0 ·

A PLAN FOR A BETTER
EDUCATIONAL SYSTEM

This book aims not to recommend policies designed to raise the United States' average PISA scores, but instead to emphasize that the PISA analyses show some weaknesses in America's public school system. The book also offers ideas for improving these weaknesses by stressing that most higher-scoring nations deal with these problems in better ways than the United States. If policymakers implement these ideas to enhance the education system, America's PISA scores will likely rise. Overemphasizing test scores as has happened in the past will worsen the American educational system because this approach interferes with the creative spirit that made America a leader in education. In addition, some nations that perform better than the United States on PISA have their own problems, including inferior methods to teaching. Therefore, American policymakers need to be selective when choosing the practices of the top performers to avoid the negative practices associated with their educational systems.

Borrowing the wrong policies from high-performing nations may raise test scores but lead to new problems. Some of the East Asian nations covered in this book, for example, experience high PISA scores, but their students endure rote methods of study, high stress levels, and cheating scandals. Additionally, international test scores have led Americans to worry unjustifiably in previous years because they were poor in predicting how the United States would fare economically. Keith Baker (2007), one of the strongest critics of international tests, argued that Americans should not be concerned with international test scores because they do not measure creativity. The knowledge they measure, he argued, is less important than the imagination needed for a country to flourish. Schools, according to Mr. Baker, should encourage imagination instead of knowledge because it is the former that creates a healthy economy. To show how poor some international tests were in determining the economic potential and creativity of a nation, Mr. Baker referred to the results of the First International Mathematics Study (FIMS) as an example. Eleven nations participated in FIMS in 1964, and the United States scored second to last. However, the American students who took the test in 1964 led the United States to a strong economy in the 21st century. Mr. Baker argued that the nations that surpassed the United States on the FIMS in the 1960s averaged per capita incomes lower than the United States' in 2002. In addition, he mentioned that the United States clobbered the countries outscoring America on the FIMMS in creativity by comparing the average number of patents issued in 2004. These nations had an average of 127 patents per million people, but the United States had 326 patents per million people (Baker, 2007). In an article in the *Los Angeles Times*, he mentioned that these accomplishments do not reflect the outcomes of a failing school system as the FIMS scores suggested but the best one in the world in the 1960s (Baker, 2008).

Lessons From the PISA Analyses

The PISA, however, differs from the FIMS in an important way, but like the FIMS, it offers little if any feedback on students' creative skills. Although the PISA may be limited in the way it measures the creativity and imagination that allow the United States to thrive economically, it is an important assessment for several reasons. First, the PISA analyses reveal major problems with the United States' education system, showing the dramatic academic gaps in achievement among different American groups of students. Second, although the United States' economy may be stronger than those of other nations, its inequalities in income are larger than those of almost all other wealthy nations (Berliner, 2013). These inequities are reflected in the PISA scores when analyzed by different socioeconomic groups. Third, although creativity may be more important than knowledge, the skills the PISA measures involve more than just knowledge because this assessment evaluates how students apply knowledge and measures workforce knowledge, not just academic content (Rutkowski, Rutkowski, & Plucker, 2014). Therefore, it is a test likely to measure economic potential more accurately than other international tests. Finally, the problems Keith Baker believed existed with the United States' educational system are consistent with the ones that PISA analyses show occur in America. For example, Mr. Baker mentioned that the real concerns in America's educational system include dilapidated schools in its inner cities and the low college graduation rates of minorities (Baker, 2007).

A Possible Crisis in Education

Although Keith Baker was correct in pointing out that Americans sometimes worry too much about test scores, researchers who say the current state of the American public school system is in need of improvement are accurate as well. Additionally, the progress other countries have made in education as the United States remained stagnant could very well enhance their economies, despite critics who doubt that a strong link exists between a country's education system and its economy.

If a link between education and the economy exists, how could America have thrived economically in the 21st century with students who scored poorly on the FIMS in the 1960s and who later never scored particularly well on international tests? This is a question that critics of international tests sometimes ask. One answer involves the lead the United States held in previous years in many other aspects of education. As I pointed out in the previous chapter, the United States had the lead in high school graduation rates and also had a very high ratio of young adults with a college degree, but other countries have surpassed it. Figure 10.1 shows that the United States has lower high school graduation rates than those of many countries.

Figure 10.1: Upper secondary graduation rates (2013)

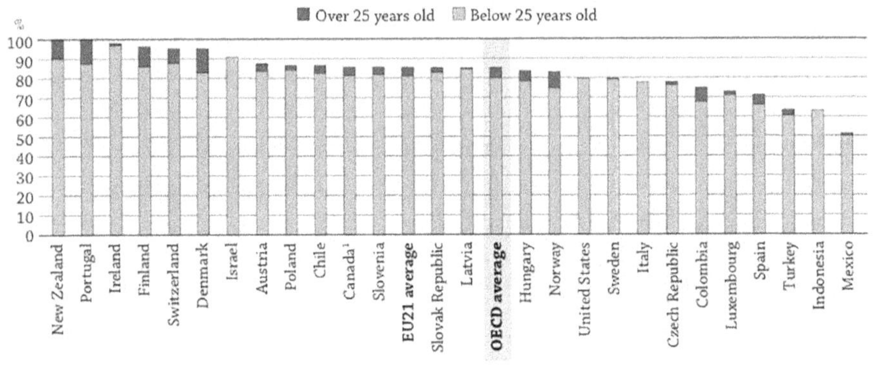

Source: OECD (2015, Chart A.2.1).

The higher percentages of high school and college graduates in previous years contributed to the strong economy the United States enjoys today. However, the United States could experience an economic decline if it fails to keep up with the progress in education other nations are making. Vivien Stewart made this point in response to scholars who question the link between a nation's education system and its economy:

> How much impact does the educational quality of a nation's schools have on economic prosperity? This is a key question. Some people argue that the relationship is not important, pointing out that despite the United States' mediocre performance on international tests since A Nation at Risk was published in the early 1980s (National Commission on Excellence in Education, 1983), the nation has still prospered economically. Although true in some respects, what this argument doesn't take into account is the time lag between the population's education levels and the country's economic output. In other words, America still enjoys a higher proportion of older adult workers with high school and college diplomas than its international counterparts. (Stewart, 2012, p. 28)

Although the extent to which high school and college graduation rates affect America's economy is debatable, it would be hard to claim that these rates have a small impact.

High school graduates typically earn more than their counterparts with less education, thereby benefitting society more as a result of their purchasing power. In addition, they are less likely to go to prison or to receive welfare services. The Alliance of Excellent Education calculated that over a span of 10 years, high school dropouts cost society over $2 trillion (Stewart, 2012). In addition, it is difficult to determine the impact between PISA test scores and the economy because the PISA was not implemented before the 21st century. Thus, it is too early to establish a link between PISA scores and nations' economies. While the poor performance of American students on the FIMS appears not to have harmed America's economy, lackluster performance on the PISA could lead to such an effect because the PISA measures workforce skills and knowledge.

One reason other countries recently made remarkable progress in education involves the reforms they made that led to high standards for teachers, competitive teacher salaries, strong teacher education programs, and improved social and educational opportunities for the poor. As many of the previous chapters pointed out, the United States has not made much progress in these areas, and its educational opportunities for the poor have declined as a result of the increase in segregated schools. If this trend continues, the United States will likely experience a gloomy future. When severe inequalities in any society exist for too long without reforms to alleviate them, the outcome is often violent (Berliner, 2013).

The crisis involving America's educational system results from other factors. As the previous chapter mentioned, the United States is currently experiencing a much greater teacher shortage problem than in past years, caused in part by the failure to supply qualified teachers in low-income areas. This concern results from multiple causes, including an increase in enrollment in schools, a decrease in enrollment in teacher preparation programs, an increase in teacher attrition rates, and the low pay that makes the teaching profession unattractive, especially in low-income areas.

Attrition rates rose by about 50% between 1989 and 2005 and remain high. With regard to student enrollment, the National Center for Education Statistics indicates that this rate has increased substantially from 1986 to 2007, followed by a steady rate from 2007 to 2015. However, the rate is projected to increase again by 2025. As for the decline in enrollment in undergraduate and graduate teacher preparation programs, this rate dropped by 35% between 2009 and 2014 (Sutcher, Darling-Hammond, & Carver-Thomas, 2016).

Although such statistics justify the enactment of major reforms, they need to be put in perspective with the rapid growth of the teacher workforce in earlier years. The teacher workforce grew at a rate considerably higher than the student enrollment growth rate in previous years. Programmatic changes implemented between the late 1980s and 2008 contributed to the growth of the teacher workforce at a rate over twice the rate of student enrollment growth (Sutcher et al., 2016).

The American public school system needs strong reforms very soon because the current teacher shortage problem is exacerbating a problem that has already worsened—the increase in the lack of educational opportunities for the poor. Schools in low-income districts typically suffer more when teacher shortage problems exist, as Chapter 9 pointed out, because qualified teachers usually take positions with wealthier districts that pay more, leading poor districts to lower their qualifications when hiring teachers. This problem in addition to the growth of segregation combined with the vast differences in income inequality between the wealthy and the poor could lead to a catastrophic outcome. As David Berliner (2013) suggested, if reforms that offer more opportunities for the poor are not implemented soon, a violent outburst will likely occur.

A Plan for Improvement

As I discussed in Chapter 1, good schools can make a difference. However, the inequalities students experience out of school usually have more impact on academic achievement than those involving the school and its teachers, simply because students spend more time out of school than in it. To narrow the achievement gap effectively, enacting policies that reduce the gap in wealth is equally if not more important than just reforming the school system. Policies need to be implemented to help low-income families have a better chance to offer their children the conditions needed to succeed. A good plan must therefore reduce inequalities in wealth *and* improve the schools low-income children typically attend.

A logical way to start is by creating policies that allow low-income children more opportunities to begin school with the conditions and skills they need for future academic success. For example, a policy could be designed to offer universal preschool programs. Research shows that underprivileged children enter kindergarten with inferior language skills that reduce their chances for academic success and that high-quality preschool programs help in reducing this gap in skills. Currently, most states are not committed to making such programs available for all students (Darling-Hammond, 2014).

Such a policy would be similar to Finland's approach to preschool. In Finland, equal and universal day care for children is guaranteed and subsidized according to income level, and almost all children (98%) participate in preschool (Chandler, 2014). Finland also uses other methods to make sure all children have a better chance to succeed before they start school, such as offering comprehensive health services. Finland's strong commitment to equity contributes to a poverty level below 4%, much lower than the United States' poverty level, which is over 20% (Sahlberg, 2012).

Finland is not the only country that recognizes the importance of early childhood education. An OECD (2017) report not only confirmed that early childhood education enhances future learning but also mentioned that many nations have increased spending on it. Unfortunately, the United States is behind other countries in providing early childhood education:

> In 2015, most countries provided free access to early childhood education to all children for at least the last year before entering primary school, though that was not the case in the U.S., where that benefit is offered only in a handful of states. (Camera, 2017, para. 9)

At $9,986 per child, the United States spends above the $7,927 average other countries spend; however, it spends considerably less of its GDP (0.4%) on preschool than average (Camera, 2017). A more important concern involves the preschools available for low-income families; like the inferior K–12 schools poor children normally attend, the preschools they enroll in are also lower in quality (Valentino, 2015).

Improved Social Policies

In reforming the preschool system, it would be wise to provide not just equal preschools but superior preschool programs for low-income children to offset the difficult conditions these students usually experience. Such schools can include more resources than other preschools. Such a practice is similar to one of Singapore's exemplary methods and would counteract the increasing inequalities low-income families have endured in recent years.

One way to implement new policies designed to fund more early childhood education opportunities, reduce income inequality, and create other programs to help the poor is by raising taxes. In comparison with other OECD countries, the United Sates has a very low tax rate. Twenty-nine countries pay a higher tax rate relative to GDP than the United States, and only two nations pay lower taxes. Some countries—such as Norway, Sweden, France, Italy, Finland, and Denmark—pay approximately 75% more, allowing their people to have free health care, unemployment support, free preschool, and even free college for those who pass a college entrance exam. Instead of paying taxes, many lucrative American corporations receive rebates (Berliner, 2013).

Some of the revenues from such a tax plan can be used for increasing summer employment opportunities for low-income youth. Youth unemployment has been a concern because the population of youth has grown in the recent past as youth employment rates have decreased. Summer employment for disadvantaged youth is beneficial because it enhances emotional development, reduces crime and violent behavior, and increases school attendance (Schwartz & Leos-Urbel, 2014). Sadly, racial inequalities pertaining to summer employment opportunities exist. For example, one study found that African American youth in Baltimore were less likely to have jobs despite applying more often than whites (Entwisle, Alexander, & Olson, 2000).

Another possibility includes creating more programs for training workers from low-income groups to provide them with the skills to get high-paying jobs. Millions of Americans live in poverty because they lack the skills employers want. Although one program—the 1998 Workforce Investment Act (WIA) Adult program—helped low-income workers, the program's funding declined, and it was not reauthorized for over a decade. This government-funded program provided low-income workers with vouchers they could use to purchase training at community colleges and private training providers. More funding for such programs can be provided than in previous years, and researchers can explore ways to improve these programs. Such a strategy would allow the United States to help the poor through vocational training programs at a level comparable with other countries. Currently, many countries including Finland, Canada, and Estonia spend more on such programs, with some countries spending 10 times as much (McConnell, Perez-Johnson, & Berk, 2014).

In addition, the government could create more incentives for states to support reducing the barriers that prevent low-income students from enrolling in and graduating from college. In comparison with the 82% of students from privileged families enrolled in college in 2010, only 52% of low-income students attended, and similar gaps exist with regard to college graduation rates (Long, 2014). Although tuition is a major barrier, inadequate academic preparation can also be an obstacle. For example, more low-income students are placed in remediation classes in college when they first enroll than students from higher socioeconomic groups (National Conference of State Legislatures, n.d.)

The requirement to take these classes makes it harder for low-income students to succeed in college for several reasons. First, students taking remedial classes usually experience delays in graduation because credit for such courses normally does not count toward graduation. Second, these delays can affect a student's eligibility for financial aid because it may expire. Third, cost is a factor because students have to pay for courses that academically prepared students take for free in high school. As a consequence, students who have to take these courses are much less likely to graduate from college, leading many types of remediation programs to fail in producing favorable outcomes. To alleviate these problems, funding can be used to implement strategies to avoid the need for remediation, improve current remediation services, and avoid inappropriate placement in college remediation classes (Long, 2014).

Another policy that can be implemented is to offer free welfare services, such as mental, dental, vision, and psychological care, at schools for the poor. Such an approach would be similar to Finland's current strategies for achieving a high percentage of students from socioeconomically disadvantaged families who do well on PISA. Schools can also offer programs for adults, including job training, health clinics, exercise facilities, and access to technology. When the school is more connected to the community through these kinds of services, a positive atmosphere develops that creates more opportunities for children to thrive physically, emotionally, and academically (Berliner, 2013).

Policies to Improve the Teaching Profession

As mentioned previously, the teacher shortage problem could worsen the already existing inequalities if not dealt with soon. Some of the policies top-performing countries implement that make them devoid of teacher shortage concerns need to be implemented in the United States. Top-performing nations such as Finland, Canada, and Singapore used specific strategies in recent decades to attract, distribute, and prepare highly skilled teachers instead of lowering standards the way the United States typically does when dealing with an inadequate supply of teachers. These strategies include implementing the following:

- Competitive salaries similar in pay with other professions, such as engineers, and equal pay regardless of the socioeconomic groups the school serves most (with incentives for hard-to-staff areas).
- Rigorous teacher education programs sponsored by the government that include extensive opportunities for practice teaching.
- Light teaching loads that allow shared planning and mentoring of beginning teachers by expert teachers.
- Collegial work settings and opportunities for ongoing professional learning (Sutcher et al., 2016).

The previous chapters in this book mentioned the stark differences between the ways top-performing nations deal with attracting, preparing, and retaining teachers and the methods the United States uses. The United States' current approach to education needs to end because if a new plan is not implemented, the country will most likely endure economic consequences, and the recent racial and social unrest will continue to expand.

In starting a new plan for improving the school system, policymakers can focus on improving teacher preparation programs. Although the United States has some outstanding programs, it also has too many that provide teachers with inadequate training. According to a study published by Michigan State University's Education Policy Center, for example, too many teacher preparation programs are not providing math teachers with the training they need:

> [T]here are reasons to be concerned about the inadequate mathematics knowledge of U.S. teachers, both at the primary and middle-school level. Although some U.S. teacher preparation programs are among the best of the world, the reality is that far too many teachers do not receive adequate mathematics training before they enter the classroom. This is a particular problem in middle school, as roughly three-fifths of such future math teachers graduate from the bottom quarter of teacher preparation programs in the U.S. This is especially disconcerting given the recent adoption of the Common Core State Standards by over forty states. In addition, our analysis reveals that the least-prepared teachers are more likely to be hired by the poorest, most-disadvantaged schools, exacerbating educational inequality. Further, despite the fact that the international primary benchmark only constitutes five courses, only a little over half of future U.S. primary teachers reported taking them. (Schmidt, Burroughs, & Cogan, 2013, p. 11)

One way to improve the rigor of teacher preparation programs is to raise their standards rather than lower them to deal with the teacher shortage problem. Many American students with strong academic credentials likely avoid majoring in education because it is perceived as an easy major that leads to a low-paying career. A recent survey, for example, found that 58% of top college students would consider a major in education if teacher preparation programs had more competitive admissions standards (Iasevoli, 2016).

To solve the concerns related to low teacher pay and low teacher preparation standards, American policymakers may not even need to model top-performing nations because two U.S. states—Connecticut and North Carolina—have already solved these problems. Solving these problems led these states to have no teacher shortage problems as well. These states invested in the teaching profession by increasing teachers' salaries and also dealt with many inequalities by enhancing pay equity across their districts.

Connecticut provided more aid to low-income districts, thereby creating more incentives for qualified teachers to work in high-need schools. These states also enhanced their teacher preparation programs and raised the standards for earning a license. For example, students in Connecticut were required to take additional training for special education, literacy, and instruction of new English learners, and North Carolina required all its public teacher education programs to be nationally accredited (Sutcher et al., 2016).

One promising aspect of ESSA is that it includes provisions for reducing inequalities. These provisions require states to create a plan that describes the steps they will take to avoid disproportionally placing ineffective, inexperienced teachers in schools that serve large numbers of students from socioeconomically disadvantaged groups. For this goal to be fulfilled, states can define what constitutes an ineffective teacher and use funding they are eligible for under ESSA to attract high-quality teachers. In addition, the federal government can enforce the aspects of ESSA that call for funding equity and teacher equity (Podolsky, Kini, Bishop, & Darling-Hammond, 2016).

Another strategy that can increase the numbers of qualified teachers involves service scholarships and loan forgiveness. Although some federal grants that provide financial incentives currently exist, compared with the top-performing nations that pay all costs for teacher preparation, the United States does little in this area. Two states that have notable programs other states can model are North Carolina and South Carolina. The North Carolina Teaching Fellows Program pays all college costs for qualified high school students who teach for several years. For over 25 years, almost 11,000 candidates have been recruited through this program. The program also attracts a higher than average percentage of minority candidates. Additionally, research on this program shows that its teachers are more effective than their counterparts in enhancing students' achievement. They are also more inclined to remain in teaching by their fifth year (Sutcher et al., 2016).

Support for new teachers also needs to improve especially in high-need areas. Research indicates that new teachers in low-income schools are less likely to have formal mentors than their peers who work for wealthier districts. Such teachers usually communicate very little with a mentor teacher about topics involving classroom management and instruction. In addition, the overall support new teachers typically get has declined in recent years as a result of budget cuts. In 2008, for example, more novice teachers had a mentor than in 2012 (Podolsky et al., 2016).

Because administrative support is a crucial component of school improvement, any plan designed to reform a school system needs to ensure that all school leaders are qualified. In fact, dissatisfaction with administrative support is often more important than any other reason that teachers offer for leaving their profession. Schools where teachers feel their administrators do not encourage them or lack a clear vision have much higher teacher turnover rates. Ensuring that all schools have strong leaders can therefore alleviate the teacher shortage problem. Teachers generally want to remain in their profession when they have school leadership that promotes an effective teaching environment and allows opportunities for them to continue to develop their skills. Regrettably, teachers working in low-income areas tend to perceive their principals as ineffective. In addition, the United States is behind other countries in its effort to recruit and train principals. Federal and state policies need to be implemented to support this crucial component of improving a school system. Only a few states currently have initiatives for this purpose (Sutcher et al., 2016).

Conclusion

Modeling the highest-scoring nations in international testing to improve the American educational system is an interesting but controversial topic. On one hand, the top-performing educational systems use outstanding practices, many of which would enhance the American system. On the other hand, cultural attitudes that contribute to high test scores are hard, sometimes impossible, to borrow. In addition, controversies exist involving the extent to which test scores predict students' future success. Finally, some top-performing nations lack the creative teaching methods that helped the United States to be recognized as the undisputed leader in education in previous years.

Despite all the controversies associated with international tests, it would be hard for anyone to justify that the gap in academic achievement these tests reveal is not harmful. It would be difficult to argue that most nations with higher test scores than the United States do not implement better policies for their low-income students, despite the problems they endure involving other aspects of education. Critics of international tests often say that test scores do not measure creativity, a crucial component of education that is believed to contribute strongly to the United States' economy. This criticism is valid because knowing and analyzing content require different skills than inventing ways to solve new problems and taking appropriate risks to run a business well. Students who simply have more academic knowledge than others are not necessarily going to have a good chance to become great authors, inventors, scientists, and artists. In order for them to have a better chance, they need to learn from great teachers who encourage creativity, or live in a society that does not penalize them for pursuing creative goals.

Unfortunately, in some East Asian nations, students tend to face negative consequences when they deviate from the rigid approach to education that requires them to score highly on the exams they need to take to go to a good university. Such an approach hinders their creative and entrepreneurial potential. In one of his books on the Chinese education system, Yong Zhao (2014) referred to a professor at Peking University who criticized China's system. This professor was critical because China had failed to produce Nobel Prize winners, despite the large numbers of students in certain areas of the country who score very highly on tests. He referred to this professor to emphasize that the PISA scores do little to measure creativity.

However, the infinitesimal number of high school students who later become Nobel Prize winners would probably achieve high PISA scores. Many of them not only go on to complete doctorates but also graduate from top universities that require superior college entrance exam scores. Such an achievement requires a strong academic record including the high test scores needed to pursue the college work many Nobel Prize winners complete at prestigious universities. For example, a study investigating different aspects of 155 Nobel laureates in physics, chemistry, and physiology/medicine who received the prize during the previous two decades indicated that most of them earned a Ph.D./M.D. and received their degrees at very competitive universities. This study found that a large number of the laureates received their degrees from the most competitive universities in the world, such as UC Berkeley, Columbia University, Massachusetts Institute of Technology (MIT), and Harvard University (Schlagberger, Bornmann, & Bauer, 2016).

The study suggests that the knowledge needed to do well on international tests is not worthless because it is a prerequisite for the creative activities that enable Nobel laureates to win this prize. This knowledge may constitute an inferior aspect of education that some East Asian nations appear to overemphasize at the expense of more important components such as creativity. But in order to have the creativity that will benefit society, students need to have basic skills and knowledge. If many low-income American students lack the skills to do well on international tests, it is a sign that America will endure more problems than it should. The best solution is to fix the unequal school system to provide underprivileged students with the education they deserve. Such an education should not only develop the skills they need to perform highly on tests like the PISA but also promote the critical thinking skills, imagination, and creativity that are characteristic of the American education system. If this goal is achieved, *all* American students will benefit and so will American society.

References

Baker, K. (2007). Are international tests worth anything? *Phi Delta Kappan*, 89(2), 101–104.

Baker, K. (2008, June 25). Low test scores, high achievement? *Los Angeles Times*. Retrieved from http://www.latimes.com/opinion/la-oew-baker25-2008jun25-story.html

Berliner, D. (2013). Effects of inequality and poverty vs. teachers and schooling on America's youth. *Teachers College Record*. Retrieved from http://www.tcrecord.org/content.asp?contentid=16889

Camera, L. (2017, June 21). U.S. trails in early childhood education enrollment. *U.S. News & World Report*. Retrieved from https://www.usnews.com/news/best-countries/articles/2017-06-21/us-falls-behind-other-developed-countries-in-early-childhood-education-enrollment

Chandler, M. A. (2014, March 4). Finland working to expand early education. *The Washington Post*. Retrieved from https://www.washingtonpost.com/local/education/finland-working-to-expand-early-education/2014/03/04/571aacf8-a3ba-11e3-8466-d34c451760b9_story.html?utm_term=.6399bbc89618

Darling-Hammond, L. (2014). What can PISA tell us about U.S. education policy? *New England Journal of Public Policy*, 26(1), 1–14.

Entwisle, D. R., Alexander, K. L., & Olson, L. S. (2000). Early work histories of urban youth. *American Sociological Review*, 65(2), 279–297.

Iasevoli, B. (2016, November 29). Higher standards urged for teacher-prep programs: Top students could improve profession. *Education Week*. Retrieved from http://www.edweek.org/ew/articles/2016/11/30/higher-standards-urged-for-teacher-prep-programs.html

Long, B. T. (2014). Addressing the academic barriers to higher education. In M. S. Kearney & B. H. Harris (Eds.), *Policies to address poverty in America* (pp. 67–76). Washington, DC: The Brookings Institution.

McConnell, S., Perez-Johnson, I., & Berk, J. (2014). Providing disadvantaged workers with skills to succeed in the labor market. In M. S. Kearney & B. H. Harris (Eds.), *Policies to address poverty in America* (pp. 97–105). Washington, DC: The Brookings Institution.

National Conference of State Legislatures. (n.d.) *Hot topics in higher education: Reforming remedial education*. Retrieved from http://www.ncsl.org/research/education/improving-college-completion-reforming-remedial.aspx

Organization of Economic Co-operation and Development. (2015). *Education at a glance 2015: OECD indicators, OECD publishing*. Paris: Organization of Economic Cooperation and Development.

Organization for Economic Co-operation and Development. (2017). *Starting strong V: Transitions from early childhood education and care to primary education*. Paris: Organization of Economic Cooperation and Development.

Podolsky, A., Kini, T., Bishop, J., & Darling-Hammond, L. (2016). *Solving the teacher shortage: How to attract and retain excellent educators*. Palo Alto, CA: Learning Policy Institute.

Rutkowski, D., Rutkowski, L., & Plucker, J. A. (2014). Should individual U.S. schools participate in PISA? *Phi Delta Kappan, 96*(4), 68–73.

Sahlberg, P. (2012). A model lesson: Finland shows us what equal opportunity looks like. *American Educator, 36*(1), 20–27.

Schlagberger, E. M., Bornmann, L., & Bauer, J. (2016). At what institutions did Nobel laureates do their prize-winning work? An analysis of biographical information on Nobel laureates from 1994 to 2014. *Scientometrics, 109*(2), 723–767.

Schmidt, W., Burroughs, N., & Cogan, L. (2013). *World class standards for preparing teachers of mathematics*. East Lansing, MI: Education Policy Center

Schwartz, A. E., & Leos-Urbel, J. (2014). Expanding summer employment opportunities for low-income youth. In M. S. Kearney & B. H. Harris (Eds.), *Policies to address poverty in America* (pp. 55–66). Washington, DC: The Brookings Institution.

Stewart, V. (2012). *A world-class education: Learning from international models of excellence and innovation*. Alexandria, VA: ASCD.

Sutcher, L., Darling-Hammond, L., & Carver-Thomas, D. (2016). *A coming crisis in teaching? Teacher supply, demand, and shortages in the U.S.* Palo Alto, CA: Learning Policy Institute.

Valentino, R. A. (2015). Will public pre-k really close achievement gaps? Gaps in prekindergarten quality between students and across states. *Center for Education Policy Analysis*. Retrieved from https://cepa.stanford.edu/sites/default/files/Valentino%20RA_Quality%20Gaps%20Paper%2015_0515.pdf

Zhao, Y. (2014). *Who's afraid of the big bad dragon? Why China has the best (and worst) education system in the world*. San Francisco, CA: Jossey-Bass.

INDEX

GLOBAL
STUDIES IN
EDUCATION

A.C. (Tina) Besley, Michael A. Peters,
Cameron McCarthy, Fazal Rizvi
General Editors

Global Studies in Education is a book series that addresses the implications of the powerful dynamics associated with globalization for re-conceptualizing educational theory, policy and practice. The general orientation of the series is interdisciplinary. It welcomes conceptual, empirical and critical studies that explore the dynamics of the rapidly changing global processes, connectivities and imagination, and how these are reshaping issues of knowledge creation and management and economic and political institutions, leading to new social identities and cultural formations associated with education.

We are particularly interested in manuscripts that offer: a) new theoretical, and methodological, approaches to the study of globalization and its impact on education; b) ethnographic case studies or textual/discourse based analyses that examine the cultural identity experiences of youth and educators inside and outside of educational institutions; c) studies of education policy processes that address the impact and operation of global agencies and networks; d) analyses of the nature and scope of transnational flows of capital, people and ideas and how these are affecting educational processes; e) studies of shifts in knowledge and media formations, and how these point to new conceptions of educational processes; f) exploration of global economic, social and educational inequalities and social movements promoting ethical renewal.

For additional information about this series or for the submission of manuscripts, please contact one of the series editors:

A.C. (Tina) Besley: t.besley@waikato.ac.nz
Cameron McCarthy: cmccart1@illinois.edu
Michael A. Peters: mpeters@waikato.ac.nz
Fazal Rizvi: frizvi@unimelb.edu.au

To order other books in this series, please contact our Customer Service Department:
    (800) 770-LANG (within the U.S.)
    (212) 647-7706 (outside the U.S.)
    (212) 647-7707 FAX

Or browse online by series:
    www.peterlang.com